T0038235

NIGHT MOTHER

21st CENTURY ESSAYS
David Lazar and Patrick Madden, Series Editors

NIGHT MOTHER

A PERSONAL AND CULTURAL
HISTORY OF *THE EXORCIST*

✝

Marlena Williams

MAD CREEK BOOKS, AN IMPRINT OF
THE OHIO STATE UNIVERSITY PRESS
COLUMBUS

Copyright © 2023 by The Ohio State University.
All rights reserved.
Mad Creek Books, an imprint of The Ohio State University Press.

Library of Congress Cataloging-in-Publication Data
Names: Williams, Marlena, 1992– author.
Title: Night mother : a personal and cultural history of The exorcist / Marlena
  Williams.
Other titles: 21st century essays.
Description: Columbus : Mad Creek Books, an imprint of The Ohio
  State University Press, [2023] | Series: 21st century essays | Includes
  bibliographical references. | Summary: "Blends personal narrative with
  cultural criticism to explore the ways The Exorcist has influenced the
  author's life and American culture, tracing stories of the film's stars and
  analyzing infamous scenes while excavating the deeper stories the film tells
  about faith, family, illness, anger, guilt, desire, and death"—Provided by
  publisher.
Identifiers: LCCN 2023007266 | ISBN 9780814258767 (paperback) | ISBN
  081425876X (paperback) | ISBN 9780814282946 (ebook) | ISBN
  0814282946 (ebook)
Subjects: LCSH: Williams, Marlena, 1992—Family. | Exorcist (Motion picture)
  | Motion pictures—History.
Classification: LCC PN1997.E95 W55 2023 | DDC 791.43/72—dc23/
  eng/20230422
LC record available at https://lccn.loc.gov/2023007266

Cover design by adam bohannon
Text design by Juliet Williams
Type set in Adobe Sabon
♾ The paper used in this publication meets the minimum requirements of the
American National Standard for Information Sciences—Permanence of Paper
for Printed Library Materials. ANSI Z39.48-1992.

CONTENTS

NOTE TO READERS

This is a work of creative nonfiction. While all the stories in this book are true, some names and identifying details have been changed to protect the privacy of the people involved.

Part 1

✛

INVOCATIONS

MERCEDES McCAMBRIDGE
EATS A RAW EGG

The human fetus begins to detect sounds from outside the womb at eighteen weeks. At this stage, the tiny bones of the middle ear can sense the vibrations of acoustic waves, which then travel down the cranial nerve to the neurons in the brain that are responsible for processing sound. The cochlea, eardrum, and ossicles are fully formed by week twenty-four. By week thirty-five, the human ear is complete. Though amniotic fluid muffles incoming sound, the fetus is highly sensitive to the world's racket. Outside noises affect fetal heart patterns, movement, and sleep. Anything above one hundred decibels is known to cause fetal stress. Parenting books therefore caution pregnant women to avoid motorcycles, gunfire, rock concerts, jet engines, and chainsaws.

The fetus is sensitive to quieter noises too. Ultrasound images have shown fetuses turning their heads ever so slightly in response to the sound of their mother's voice. When the mother speaks, the sound is amplified as it hurtles down her body and reverberates through her bones. For months the fetus floats in a pool echoing with its mother's bodily cacophony. It can hear the sounds of her heartbeat, her breathing, her digestion. It can hear her walking, chewing, drinking, coughing, vomiting, burping, laughing, crying, swearing, and screaming.

Because the average human scream reaches about 110 decibels, women are also advised to avoid screaming while pregnant. This, of course, is an odd bit of advice, as women are so rarely encouraged to scream at all.

•

One of the most shocking things about the 1973 horror classic *The Exorcist* isn't what you see but what you hear. Early audiences were as terrified by the sounds the possessed little girl made as they were by the horrible things she was made to do. In fact, the sounds were terrifying precisely because they were coming out of the mouth of a round-faced twelve-year-old girl. A child couldn't possibly make noises like that.

At the height of her possession, bronchial wheezes and guttural moans seep out of the young girl's mouth as if hell itself is yawning awake. The voice—like a dying animal clawing its way out of a smoke-stripped throat—isn't the voice of a young innocent whose vocal cords seem primed for giggles and song. This is the devil's bark. A child couldn't possibly say those horrible words either. *Your mother sucks cocks in hell. Stick your cock up her ass you motherfucking worthless cock sucker. Your cunting daughter.* Abominations, words not meant for a child's lips.

Though *The Exorcist* is often defined by its most well-known images—the spinning head, the spewing vomit, the thrusting crucifix, the priest standing beneath the streetlamp at 3600 Prospect Street—much of its enduring horror is thanks to the career-defining vocal performance of Mercedes McCambridge. No, little Linda Blair did not make those blood-curdling noises herself. Just as a stunt double named Eileen Dietz was brought in to perform the more gruesome physical acts required by the script, director William Friedkin enlisted McCambridge to give voice to the demon Pazuzu. The performance would become so iconic that it obliterated everything else about McCambridge's storied career. When she died in 2004, at the age of eighty-seven, her *USA Today* obituary referred to her in its headline as "*The Exorcist* actress," which must have caused some confusion among readers who saw it and assumed that Linda Blair, not McCambridge, had suddenly passed on.

Orson Welles once called McCambridge "the world's greatest living radio actress." Born Carlotta Mercedes Agnes McCambridge in Joliet, Illinois, she rose to prominence during the 1930s on radio programs like *Lights Out, Inner Sanctum, Midnight Murder,* and *Radio Mystery Theater.* McCambridge was the kind of star who needn't be seen to make an impact, though when she was seen—on Broadway or alongside Hollywood icons like Elizabeth Taylor, Joan Crawford, and Rock Hudson—she held her own. McCambridge won the Oscar for Best Supporting Actress in 1950 for her role as Sadie Burke in *All the Kings Men* and was nominated again seven years later for her performance in *Giant,* the last of James Dean's films. She quickly gained a reputation for playing tough, strong-willed broads who spoke their minds, shunning the type of whispery, busty glamor-girl parts that might have granted her fame eternal. Of course, with her slightly pointed nose and short, dark hair, McCambridge was far from a Hollywood bombshell. But she didn't need to be—not when she had that voice. It was a one-of-a-kind voice, simultaneously trembling and sonorous, with a haunting crackle that could at any point explode into something howling and wild.

McCambridge's heavy drinking likely gave her voice some of its distinctive bite. Her addiction contributed to two divorces, several hospitalizations, and a midcareer slump that left her grasping for bit parts in episodes of *Bewitched* and *Lost in Space.* Though she was in recovery by the beginning of the 1970s, it must have come as a relief and a surprise when Friedkin offered her a role in his new horror film. She would not appear on screen, he told her, but it would be her voice that brought the demon to life. Friedkin has said that McCambridge was perfect because her voice was "neutral, neither male nor female."

McCambridge was fifty-six when she stepped into the sound studio. Before recording, she chain-smoked cigarettes and gargled a noxious combination of raw eggs and whiskey, a sulfurous cocktail made all the more potent in light of McCambridge's addiction. McCambridge, a devoted Catholic, demanded that her priest remain in the studio at all times to help her fight the demon's call. While recording, she was strapped to a chair, her arms and legs bound so she could barely move. McCambridge has said she didn't want to be tied up; Fredkin maintains it was all her idea. Whoever made the decision, it is this that gives the voice its vengeful, straining rasp. It is the sound of a human animal struggling against its restraints, raging to break through the broken body that contains it. If you listen closely, there are layers to the sound. Two, three, four different strains often seem to echo at once. The demon wheezes and growls and screams. It laughs and it cries. There is something jarringly comical about it too. At times, McCambridge seems to adopt a refined British accent. At other times, a feral snarl. And underneath it all, the foul bite of whiskey, hot and burning on the tongue.

"It wasn't hard for me to imagine the rage," McCambridge said in the documentary *The Fear of God: The Making of The Exorcist*. "You see, if it's this close in me right here, and I'm only a human being, it's that close in everybody."

•

McCambridge had one child, a son, born in 1941. She was

only twenty-three when she had him; her career was just beginning. That son, John Markle, would grow up to become an eccentric futures trader with a PhD in economics and a penchant for wearing purple shoes. His coworker at the Arkansas investment firm Stephens Inc. alleged that Markle once threatened to kill him with an AK-47 and then theatrically loaded the trunk of his car with guns to prove he had the firepower to do so.

Markle was like his mother in at least one obvious way. His constant drinking and smoking made him an unhealthy man, so unhealthy that he needed a sextuple bypass at age forty-three. In the wake of the surgery, McCambridge briefly relocated to Arkansas so she could be close to her ailing son and his family in Little Rock, even though this meant taking a break from her newfound work at a nonprofit treatment center for men and women struggling with addiction.

While working at Stephens Inc., Markle opened a secret bank account in his mother's name, forging her signature and embarking on a five-year embezzlement scheme that would eventually end in his firing. Markle had been arrested once before—for public intoxication and soliciting a sex worker— but this is when things finally began to spiral beyond his control. When the shocked and enraged McCambridge refused to cooperate in the restitution proceedings that might have spared her son from criminal prosecution, Markle snapped.

On a stormy, lightening-gouged November morning in 1987, Markle took a pair of guns, possibly out of the trunk of his car, and shot his wife, his two young daughters, and then, with one gun pointed on either side of his head, himself. At the scene of the crime, police found a rubber "old man" mask, the drooping beige kind with wrinkles and a creepy grin, which they speculated Markle might have been wearing when he killed his family. News reports made much of the fact that a copy of A *Nightmare on Elm Street*—a supernatural horror story which traces the grizzly trajectory of murder back to the sins of the mother—was found in Markle's VCR at the time of the murder.

Police also discovered a blood-splattered letter Markle had left for his mother in which he simultaneously took responsibility for the crime and blamed it on her. In the bitter note, Markle wrote, "You were never around much when I needed you, so now I and my whole family are dead—so you can have the money . . . 'Night, Mother."

One can only imagine what the grief-stricken McCambridge must have felt when she read her dead son's letter. Was it guilt? Sorrow? Anger? Perhaps McCambridge knew what many of us learn eventually: how easy it is to blame our mothers for our problems, to pin our every downfall or misfortune on them. It's a bitter concoction to swallow, knowing that our mothers won't always be there when we call, that they, too, are fighting their own private demons, sometimes bound by a darkness they cannot escape or control. It must have weighed heavily on Markle too, hearing his own mother wail and bark and scream for the entire world to hear. So few of our mothers ever show us what they are capable of, or dare to lay bare the raw pain and rage clawing at their hearts.

MY MOTHER AND
THE EXORCIST

A woman is startled awake by a loud sound. The first thing to flash through her mind as she jolts upright in in bed is *My daughter.* She pulls on a robe and rushes down the hall to the room where her daughter rests. She finds her there, sleeping peacefully, but all is not as she left it. The window is open, blowing in frigid fall air. Light from the streetlamp below streams into the room. The drapes flap in the cool dawn breeze. The sheets on the bed have been yanked down, leaving her daughter's prone body exposed to the morning cold. *Strange,* the mother thinks, but nothing more. She closes the window and rewraps the covers tightly around her sleeping child. She kisses her forehead, tells her she loves her, and tiptoes out of the room.

My mother rarely told me stories about her life. I think she considered talking about herself an indulgence, a selfish hogging of the air. The things she did tell me were closer to off-hand comments than fully fleshed recollections, opaque statements made in passing never to be elaborated upon again. A college boyfriend who died in a car crash. Her days spent inserting catheters in the ICU. The time she flipped off a stranger for swerving into a parking spot that was clearly hers. How he followed her through the shadowy parking garage, thrust his own middle finger into her face, and growled, "I'll poke your god damn eye out."

As a child, I clung to whatever stories she offered, hazy snapshots plucked from her memory that have only become hazier when filtered through the cluttered corridors of my own. Over a decade since her death, I still find myself sifting through the scattered shards of narrative she left behind, hoping that eventually I will assemble enough broken pieces to build something whole.

One of these stories, however, has remained as clear to me as it was the first time I heard it, and that is the story of my mother and *The Exorcist*.

Before watching *The Exorcist* was even a vaguely plausible option for my childhood self, my mother banned me from ever seeing it. It was just one of the rules of life. Don't talk to strangers. Don't cross the street without first looking both ways. Don't eat the raw cookie dough off the spatula. And don't watch *The Exorcist*.

The movie had scarred her when she snuck off to see it at age fourteen against her own mother's wishes, and she felt certain it would scar me too. Not just scare. Scar. The distinction is important. Scare implies momentary fright. Scar leaves a mark. Though I had no conception that a movie could bring anything but magic and joy, had only ever found delight on the other side of TriStar's winged horse and 20th Century Studio's spotlight and drums, I heeded my mother's warning. It was something about the way she said those words. "Don't ever watch *The Exorcist*." There was a desperation beneath them. A plea.

When *The Exorcist*—a film about the possession of a twelve-year-old girl named Regan MacNeil—premiered in the winter of 1973, my grandmother Marlene banned my mother from ever seeing it. Marlene died of a brain tumor shortly before I was born, but I know she was a deeply religious woman who chain-smoked Pall Malls and swore like a sailor. My mother told me that Marlene liked to drive her kids to school while still wearing her bathrobe and curlers, exhaust sputtering from the pipes of their clunker car and smoke curling off the tip of her extralong cigarette. To Marlene, a conservative Catholic living on a cattle farm in a rural Oregon town, *The Exorcist* was not just blasphemous but dangerous, a movie that would corrupt the mind—and perhaps even the soul—of anyone who saw it.

Mothers all across the country were banning their children from seeing *The Exorcist* in 1973. In Pauline Kael's scathing review of the film, after lampooning its "crushing blunt wittedness" and "shallowness that acts to be taken seriously," she asks, "How does one exorcise the effects of a movie like this?" She then answers her own question: "There is no way." On live TV, after his opening monologue about the Nixon White House tapes and before his interview with *The Exorcist*'s best-selling author and Academy Award–winning screenwriter, William Peter Blatty, Johnny Carson dourly warned his viewers, "Children under fifteen shouldn't see the film. It is a little too powerful for them. It could have a great effect on a child that may have a few problems to begin with. . . . It's an exciting picture but . . . don't go if you are too young."

The Exorcist arrived at a particularly raw moment in our nation's history, as truly significant works tend to do. The film premiered against the backdrop of the Watergate hearings and *Roe v. Wade,* of the spiraling Vietnam War and the first wave of POWs returning to American shores, of student protests and *Deep Throat* and *The Dark Side of the Moon* and Erica Jong's proverbial "zipless fuck." It was a manic period of reckoning after the chaos and revolution of the 1960s, the start of a riotous and disillusioned decade when America could no longer cling naively to the self-image, shiny and supreme, it had cherished for so long. Mark Kermode perhaps said it best in his book on *The Exorcist*: "For the first time in a mainstream movie, audiences witnessed the graphic desecration of everything that was considered wholesome and good about the fading American dream: the home, the family, the church, and most shockingly, the child."

The Exorcist seemed to prove America's worst fears about its fracturing national identity. Up until then, the evil America had faced, or at least thought it had faced, had always been far away: Communists, the war in Europe, space aliens, the atomic bomb. Now, from a certain frame of reference, it seemed that something corrupt and wanton had invaded the country, eroding its faith, perverting its citizens, devastating its cities, and turning its children into angry, godless, drug-addled others. Never mind the very real evils the United States was committing outside its borders, in Cambodia and Chile and Vietnam. Never mind the very real evils America had been committing against people within its own borders for centuries. If, as Robin Wood argued in "An Introduction to the American Horror Film," scary movies are society's "collective nightmare," then *The Exorcist* spoke to a very specific ideological crisis tearing at the heart of the nation.

By the time *The Exorcist* premiered in 1973, enough cultural groundwork had been laid to make fear of the devil something pressing and real. Satanic classics like *Rosemary's Baby* and *The Devil Rides Out* premiered only a few years before *The Exorcist* hit screens. Some musicians, like Jimmy Page, who notoriously purchased a mansion in the Scottish

Highlands where he could practice the black magic of Allister Crowley in peace, openly dabbled in the occult; they sang odes to Satan for millions of fans to hear, but only sometimes, and only if you played the records backward. In 1972 Michael Warnke published *The Satan Seller,* a memoir recounting his violent, sex-filled years as a high priest in a satanic cult and his eventual conversion to Evangelical Christianity. Though the memoir has since been debunked, it quickly became a bestseller in religious circles and jumpstarted Warnke's successful career as a prominent Christian comic. The same year Warnke published his memoir, American evangelist Hal Lindsey's *Satan Is Alive and Well on Planet Earth* hit shelves, warning readers that Satan had not been defeated, he had merely changed clothes.

Over in Europe, the Catholic Church helped to stoke these fears with a series of eerie proclamations about the continued presence of the devil in the world. On November 15, 1972, Pope Paul VI issued this statement:

> Evil is not merely a lack of something, but an effective agent, a living spiritual being, perverted and perverting. A terrible reality. . . . We know that this dark and disturbing spirit really exists and that he still acts with treacherous cunning; he is the secret enemy that sows terrors and misfortunes in human history. The question of the Devil, and the influence he can exert on individual persons as well as communities[,] . . . is a very important chapter of Catholic doctrine which is given little attention today, though it should be studied again.

In no obscure terms, the Pope's declaration reaffirmed the existence of the devil as a real and concrete being, not just some biblical idea about evil or lust or indulgence but a dangerous living entity hell-bent on perverting humanity's pure and noble nature. The statement worked to confirm what Wood calls America's "inherently apocalyptic destiny." A declaration specially designed to breed fear and unease, to coax steadily dwindling church congregations back into the pews.

Fear had its advantage at the polls too. After all, it was in part the Evangelical Protestants who helped propel Nixon to victory in 1968 on his promise of restoring law and order to the nation's beleaguered cities, a not-so-veiled reference to the uprisings that rocked places like Detroit, Chicago, and Baltimore near the end of the sixties. By 1973 the bitter backlash to America's leftward swing had begun, and leaders on the right were quickly catching on to the potent political power of latent white resentment and fear. Upon accepting the Republican nomination, Nixon added further fuel to the apocalyptic fire, bluntly ignoring the underlying causes of unrest—poor housing, institutionalized unemployment, and rampant police brutality—in favor of the flashy political opportunities such race-baiting rhetoric has always offered our nation's leaders.

"As we look at America, we see cities enveloped in smoke and flame," Nixon said at the Republican National Convention in Miami as protests erupted in Liberty City just miles away. "We hear sirens in the night."

•

My mother grew up far away from the cultural and political tumult, in Canby, Oregon, a small, mostly white town with a population of about four thousand in 1973. It was the type of town where you believed what you heard on TV. If a politician told you that our nation was under siege, you believed him. You locked your doors at night.

She was a cheerleader in high school, spending her Friday nights dancing in front of the bleachers in her cerulean blue and canary yellow Canby Cougar's uniform. Tall and lean, she played volleyball until she injured her knee, the surgery leaving a long scar zippered across her kneecap. In place of sports, she began riding horses. She even had her own: an Arabian named Rodack. In the old pictures I have found of my teenage mother, she wears a green swimsuit and smiles at a lake surrounded by fir trees. She stands in a dreary parking lot in front of a VW van wearing a cable-knit sweater, her hair tied back with a purple ribbon.

I know she spent an afternoon vomiting over the side of Molalla River Bridge after she tried a wad of her brother David's tobacco, and I know that her first kiss took place in the bed of David's pickup truck while Don McLean's "American Pie" played over the radio, a scene so good that I half suspect she made it up. These images—the farm and the cheerleading uniform, the horses and the pickup truck—are the images I have of my mother's youth, a simple and hearty version of white American life that, to some, might have seemed imperiled when *The Exorcist* took over theaters that Christmas in 1973.

My mother went and saw *The Exorcist* despite her mother's demands. Maybe seeing it was her own small act of a defiance, her first guilty and tentative act of adolescent individuation. How could she not take part in a generation-defining cultural moment? It must have felt like everyone was seeing *The Exorcist* that winter.

The film was mythical before it even premiered, what with all those tabloid and trade stories about a doomed production and a cast and crew steadily descending into madness. Fresh off his Oscar win for *The French Connection*, director William Friedkin took a cue from the Hitchcock playbook and did what he could to play up the film as cursed, waging what he referred to as a "campaign of disinformation" against the public (which also doubled as a convenient cover for the film's historic production delays). To build up suspense before audiences first saw *Psycho* in 1960, Hitchcock had issued a very specific set of demands to theaters, which included refusing reentry to any person who left the cinema after the movie began, playing an eerie voiceover through loudspeakers while ticketholders waited in line, and placing a sign in the foyer reading "Please don't spoil the ending. It's the only one we have."

Friedkin took this a step further, building up the intolerable suspense long before *The Exorcist* had even premiered. He told the press that inexplicable "magnetic fields" had covered the set, that no wires or pulleys were used during the film's famous levitation scene, and that strange images appeared on the film stock long after the scenes had already been shot. It was all part of Friedkin's plan, as Mark Kermode writes, "to make the piano wires suspending the actress disappear by simply telling the audience they weren't there in the first place."

Beyond Friedkin's calculated campaign of disinformation, there were rumors that Linda Blair, the young actress playing the possessed child Regan MacNeil, suffered from debilitating nightmares and regular nervous breakdowns during the entirety of production. Such an intense role, the stories went, was simply too much for a young innocent to handle. Friedkin kept the replica Georgetown house that served as the film's set at below freezing temperatures so that he could capture the actors' breath hovering in the air. Contact lenses froze on eyeballs, pipes burst, expensive cameras dripped with ice, and some even say snow fell on the set. Eventually, ice met fire when the entire set burned to the ground in an electrical blaze, on a Sunday of all days. Not long after, the new set's sprinkler system broke, causing flooding and a two-week delay. Some have even said that during filming, the crew hired a real exorcist to cleanse the studio of the supernatural darkness that seemed to have derailed production.

Then there were the deaths. Jack MacGowran, who plays the lecherous movie director Burke Dennings, died from the flu at age fifty-four, one week after completing his own death scenes for the film. Vasiliki Maliaros, who plays Father Karras's sick mother, also died the same year she finished filming. The son of Jason Miller, who plays Father Karras, died in a motorcycle accident shortly after wrapping. There were other, more peripheral deaths—Linda Blair's grandfather and Max von Sydow's brother—and several serious injuries, including lost fingers and broken bones. Years later, Paul Bateson, who plays the radiological technician in one of the film's most hard-to-watch scenes, was convicted of murdering several gay men throughout Manhattan.

On top of all of this, magazines reported that director William Friedkin and author-screenwriter William Peter Blatty feuded from start to finish, causing unwarranted standstills during both shooting and postproduction. Though the tension between Friedkin and Blatty was likely exaggerated, it is true that they had differing visions of the film. Blatty intended *The Exorcist* to be a deeply and overtly spiritual work, a story that affirmed the existence of God in our midst, while Friedkin insisted on keeping the meaning of his film opaque. He wasn't trying to convert anyone—he was trying to make a blockbuster, at whatever cost. A film that was supposed to wrap in 105 days ended up taking 200, and the budget skyrocketed from a reasonable $4 million to $8 million, then to $12 million. Even in a decade when the budgets of films and the size of the director's egos were steadily growing, this seemed like self-indulgent Hollywood excess. By the time the film finally hit theaters, it was already notorious.

Once *The Exorcist* premiered, people stood in line for hours in the frigid December cold to see the movie that was reportedly inciting mass hysteria around the globe. There were reports of people fainting and vomiting, of the film inducing heart attacks and miscarriages, of crowds leaving the theater shaking and screaming. Janitors worked overtime mopping up vomit from the aisles. In Berkeley, a man threw himself at the screen in a misguided attempt to "get the demon," the twisted opposite of early film goers who reportedly stampeded away from a screening of *L'Arrivée d'un train en gare de La Ciotat* in 1896, terrified that the train barreling across the screen was going to break forth and crash into them. Four women in Toronto were supposedly so disturbed by the film that they were subsequently confined to psychiatric care wards. Within weeks of the film's release, there was a marked increase in the number of people seeking psychiatric help, attending church, and, perhaps not surprisingly, calling priests to perform exorcisms.

West Germany banned the film because a nineteen-year-old boy named Rainer Hertrampf shot himself with an automatic rifle shortly after seeing it. When a sixteen-year-old English boy named John Power died the day after seeing *The Exorcist,* a heavily publicized inquest couldn't help but connect the two. Even when it was revealed that he died because of an epileptic attack, the image of a seizing teen felt a little too close to the film to fully ease the public's suspicions. Almost a year later, in October 1974, a nine-year-old girl was murdered by a teenager in York who then used *The Exorcist* as part of his defense. "It was not really me that did it," he said. "There was something inside me. It has been ever since I saw that film *The Exorcist.* I felt something take possession of me. It has been in me ever since."

It is true that some of these stories might be pure hyperbole. It is also true that movies have been provoking intense audience reaction since the art form began. Tod Browning's 1932 film, *Freaks,* sparked such controversy that it was pulled from many theaters and Browning's career more or less ruined. In 1971, *The Clockwork Orange* famously inspired youths across Britain to commit acts of "ultra-violence" similar to those carried out by Alex and his droogs. *Taxi Driver* inspired John Hinckley's Jr.'s attempt to assassinate Ronald Reagan in a twisted bid for Jodi Foster's affection, and someone called in a bomb threat to a showing of *The Last Tango in Paris* in Montclair, New Jersey, apparently out of disgust for the film's graphic sex scenes. One year after *The Exorcist* premiered, some audiences were so disgusted by the *Texas Chainsaw Massacre* that they threatened to sue any theater that screened it. More recent movies like *Antichrist, 127 Hours, The Passion of the Christ,* and *Irréversible* are also famous for reportedly making audience members vomit, cry, and leave the theaters in a sickened rage.

Still, there is something specific about the way *The Exorcist* terrified and shocked people in 1973. Two years later, a psychologist named James Bozzuto published a paper in *The Journal of Nervous Mental Disorders* calling the audience reactions a form of "cinematic neurosis." It didn't so much create new neurosis, Bozzuto argued, as trigger those that already existed in the psyche, latent and waiting to be released.

Some people called *The Exorcist* a sacrilegious and dangerous film. Others, like *Catholic News,* praised the film's spirituality, echoing in less snide terms Pauline Kael's statement that *The Exorcist* was "the biggest recruiting poster the Catholic Church has had since the sunnier days of *Going My Way* and *The Bells of St Mary's.*" In Britain, the Christian Festival of Light Lobby picketed screenings and handed out leaflets warning of the evil and darkness the film would unleash upon humanity if viewed by too many. In Tunisia, on the other hand, the film was banned on the grounds that it was a piece of "unjustified propaganda for Christianity."

●

The night she saw *The Exorcist*, my mother snuck out of her bedroom window, crawled across the roof, and scrambled down a tree to the dark ground below. Her friend was waiting for her in a car at the end of the long gravel driveway. My mother climbed in, and they drove to whatever dingy, one-room cinema was showing *The Exorcist* for three dollars a ticket that winter. Though it was Christmastime, the red and green lights that once twinkled from Canby homes had gone dark. With the oil crisis in full swing, Christmas trees all around the nation—from Canby to the White House—shone a little less brightly that year, yet another symbol of Christianity's steadily dimming light.

My mother always left the actual details of the film more or less blank, reducing it to the images we all associate with *The Exorcist*: pea-green vomit, a little girl's head doing a 360, and something very, very bad happening with a crucifix. It wasn't so much the things my mother said about the film that frightened me as it was the look she got in her eyes when she said them. For my mother, and for teenage girls everywhere, it must have been deeply destabilizing to see such a brutal depiction of adolescent female transformation, to be so baldly confronted with what the world thought of you and your steadily changing body and mind. It was the kind of thing that could smack a curious young girl back into pliant submission.

"It was the most frightening thing I have ever seen in my life," she told me. "I wanted to scream and run out of the theater, but I couldn't move. The whole placed seemed colder than normal. My breath just hovered in the air. I swear to God there was something else in that room, sitting there with all of us. I could feel it. I still can."

After seeing *The Exorcist,* my mother lay awake in bed, night after night, staring at her ceiling and waiting for the devil to rush into her body. She sat, red eyed and pale faced, at the breakfast table, gazing off into space and neglecting to touch the runny eggs and black toast her mother had prepared. She was still thinking about that horrible little girl and all of the disgusting things she'd been forced to say and do. She was thinking about the way Regan snarled and barked like a feral dog, and how the worse she got, the further everyone in her life backed away.

Marlene sat across from her in a frilly meringue-colored bathrobe with her elbow propped up on the table and a cigarette between her fingers, eyeing her fourteen-year-old daughter with stony suspicion.

Without asking, Marlene knew, the way all mothers know.

One night, after a week of fraught insomnia, my mother was so exhausted that she finally fell asleep. As soon as she drifted off, Marlene snuck into her room and walked over to her bed. The moonlight washing over her face, she leaned down close and began speaking to her sleeping daughter.

"Hello, Mary," Marlene whispered. "Did you go see *The Exorcist* last Friday night even though I told you not to?"

A pause, as if even my mother's subconscious sensed punishment looming.

"Yes, Mother," my mother finally answered in a dull drone. "I did."

I imagine Marlene nodding slowly and grinning in satisfaction.

"Good," she said. "We'll talk about it in the morning."

Marlene confronted my mother over breakfast the next day, informing her that they'd had a very interesting conversation the night before. My mother collapsed into tears. She promised to go to confession and say the rosary every night and wear a crucifix around her neck. She would do anything, she said, anything to get that horrible movie out of her head.

Marlene held my mother in her arms, rubbed my mother's back, and ran her fingers through her long auburn hair. Much to my mother's surprise, Marlene did not drag her off to the nearest priest or lock her in her bedroom to ponder her sins in silence. Seeing *The Exorcist* and living with its images haunting her mind must have seemed like punishment enough.

•

Four years after she saw *The Exorcist,* my mother left Canby to attend Oregon State University in Corvallis. There, she joined a sorority and fell in love with a boy who would later die.

Though I do not know his name, I have seen his picture. I found it in my mother's closet, the two of them smiling and wearing party hats, a string of shiny letters spelling out HAPPY BIRTHDAY behind them. The boy looks to be in his midtwenties, with dark hair, a prominent nose, and spots of stubble around his pale chin. His brown eyes are red and slightly glassy, as if he were a little drunk or stoned. He is wearing a cream-colored jersey-knit sweater with a block of red, blue, and mustard-colored stripes around the torso. *Cute,* I thought when I first found the photo. *Exactly the type of man I would find attractive today.* Intwined in each other's arms, they look young and happy, though slightly awkward, as if they hadn't yet had time to grow into their love. I imagine my mother, with her shining red hair and light brown trousers, standing up on a wooden chair to hang the rainbow letters before he arrived.

After college, my mother traveled around Europe with her friend Sherri—Paris, Rome, Capri—before moving to Portland for nursing school. She got a job at the intensive care unit of St. Vincent's Hospital, where she spent her days hurrying through the smell of antiseptic and steel, carrying sloshing pans of vomit and administering an endless drip of brownish liquid into the veins of sick men and women. It was her job, she'd tell me, to insert the catheters into the patients. During these years, my mother lived alone. She wore a crucifix around her neck even while she slept, content that God, and her rottweiler, Brit, would keep her safe.

At thirty, she met my father, Bill, in a Mexican restaurant. He was a cheery, sandy-haired man from Los Gatos, California, whose father had once worked as a landscaper on Alfred Hitchcock's Scott's Valley estate. After two years, they got married and bought a house in the suburbs with a wallpapered kitchen, wood-paneled basement, and a pool in the backyard. The decision to quit nursing came easily—she was ready to be a wife and a mother. Not long after the wedding, Marlene died from cancer, a disease that had first manifested in her breast but soon snaked its way into her brain. A year later, still grieving her own mother's death, my mother gave birth to me.

Like her mother before her, she forbade me from ever seeing *The Exorcist*. Like her, I would see it anyway.

I was eight years old when I first caught a glimpse of *The Exorcist*. My mother and I were sitting on the couch in our basement watching TV when it flashed on the screen: a little girl crawling down a staircase in a backbend while her mother looks on in horror. It was there, and then it disappeared, my mother clutching the remote control in her hand as the screen blipped to black. Her hair, I remember clearly, had only just started to grow back after she'd lost it all undergoing treatment for the disease that had killed her own mother less than a decade before.

I now know that what I saw was likely a trailer for the film's highly anticipated twenty-fifth anniversary rerelease—advertised as "the version you've never seen before"—in which the infamous "spider walk" that Friedkin had cut from the 1973 original was reinserted in order to help restore screenwriter Blatty's spiritual vision to the film. When Friedkin and Blatty were preparing for the rerelease, they were faced with a question: *The Exorcist* was radical for 1973, but would it be radical for 2000? Perhaps what had once made *The Exorcist* so shocking—the dirty language, the single parent, the masturbation, the urination, the subliminal images, the dying priests—wouldn't shock audiences a quarter century later. Special effects had developed a lot since the seventies. Certainly all the head spinning and pea soup would look laughably dated now. If Friedkin feared the wires were visible in 1973, then certainly they would be impossible to ignore twenty-five years later.

In the spider-walk scene, Regan climbs down the staircase on all fours. Her back is impossibly arched so that her stomach vaults toward the ceiling and the crown of her head nearly grazes the steps below. It almost resembles the Wheel pose in yoga, or a move you might see a gymnast do for a second or two on a balance beam. It certainly doesn't look like something the average human body should do, at least not for too long. The movement is less of a crawl than a frantic scurry, jittery and jarring, like the shadowy movements of the arachnid after which it is named. When Regan reaches the foot of the stairs, she vomits out a spigot spray of bright red blood, her neck still bent skyward. In an extended version of the scene that you can find online, Regan then rights herself, wild eyed, and flicks her pointed tongue in and out before dashing toward the front door on her hands and knees.

The cut scene had been whispered about among cinephiles and horror fans for years, but when the new edition finally premiered, responses were mixed. Viewers lampooned the out-of-date special effects, the disturbing bestial imagery, and the bald intent to terrify without nuance or ingenuity. Roger Ebert, who generally liked the original version of the film and even participated in a shot-by-shot analysis of it at the Hawaii Film Festival, called the spider walk a "distracting stunt" and "gratuitous." There are some undeniable problems with the scene, the most obvious being that the actress climbing down the staircase in the backbend clearly isn't Linda Blair. Some critics and fans also argued that this scene—the only one in which the fully possessed Regan emerges from the icy confines of her bedroom—disrupted the visual continuity and claustrophobic mood of the film. More positive critiques took Regan's emergence from the bedroom as evidence that she could and would spread her evil to the outside world, thus explaining why she is kept in restraints for the rest of the film.

The brief shot of the spider walk terrified my eight year old self, and, even all those years later, I think it terrified my mother too. The myth of the film was in the room there with us, a fear passed down through the generations like belief. Fear, like disease, can mutate and spread. When *The Exorcist* first terrified my mother at fourteen, I wonder if she saw in it the threat of her own impending female monstrousness, her own failures at goodness and love. When she saw *The Exorcist* as a mother herself, only recently recovered from a disease so often associated with evil itself ("a demonic enemy," Susan Sontag once called cancer), perhaps she was haunted by the memory of another kind of bodily degradation, or by the looming possibility that the thing you love most in the world, the child you are holding right there in your arms, will one day come to hate you, maybe even to destroy you.

"It's just a movie," my mother said.

But it didn't matter that *The Exorcist* was just a movie.

That phrase meant nothing to me. I couldn't separate myself from what was happening on the screen any more than I could separate what was happening on the screen from what was happening in real life. It being "just a movie" didn't make it any less terrifying or alive. I could still see its images and hear its sounds. I could still reach out and touch the TV screen with my hands, feel its warmth and buzz on my fingertips, watch the bright colors flash through the translucent skin on my palms.

I didn't sleep that night. I spent the next eight hours, and countless sleepless nights thereafter, awake in bed, eyes flicking back and forth between the crucifix hanging above my door and the hallway leading toward the staircase, waiting for the little girl to ascend it in a backbend and come for me. I didn't just fear the little girl; I feared becoming her too. Now that I had seen the darkness my mother had warned me about so many times before, I was convinced that some latent badness, some curdled thing deep inside of me, would be unleashed and I would be helpless to control it. I came to see myself as pre-possessed, as a body and a mind waiting to be destroyed.

•

The Exorcist is a film haunted by dead mothers. Both director William Friedkin and screenwriter William Peter Blatty were notoriously obsessed with their mothers and had lost them shortly before production began. Friedkin once described his mother, who fled pogroms in the Ukraine to become an operating room nurse in Chicago, as "a saint . . . like Florence Nightingale." Blatty was raised in what he called "comfortable destitution" by a deeply religious single mother who made ends meet by peddling quince and jams in the streets of Manhattan, once even offering a jar to Franklin Delano Roosevelt.

During the filming of *The Exorcist*, when Blatty wasn't hectoring Friedkin about the film's abhorrent lack of religiosity, he was at a sound studio trying to get in touch with his dead mother. He had started recording what he believed were the disembodied voices of the dead with the guidance of a book called *Breakthrough: An Amazing Experiment in Electronic Communication with the Dead* by Latvian psychologist Konstantin Raudive.

Apparently, on one of these recorded tapes, you can hear the crackling voice of Blatty whispering again and again, "Mother. Mother. If you are there, come."

•

At age fourteen, I transformed into someone foul mouthed and sullen, prone to angry outbursts and overcome by the desire to be left alone. My mother and I fought often in those days, alternating between bitter screaming matches and lengthy periods of icy, impenetrable silence. My mother was infamous for her cold shoulders; they lasted for weeks, and no amount of crying, begging, or apologizing could put a stop to them. When her cancer returned after a period of remission, it did not soften me to her as one might expect. Our relationship had fractured too much by that point for such tenderness. Her illness only left me feeling frightened and confused. Sometimes, my sick mother would look at me and shake her head. "If only I could film you right now," she'd say, "you'd be ashamed of what you see."

I convinced myself that I'd become the loathsome little girl I'd sworn never to be, someone whose anger and dissatisfaction and pain was not a natural response to the world around her but an unforgivable defect, a sign of some inner wickedness I couldn't control. I dismissed religion. I kept the crucifixes my mother gave me tangled thoughtlessly in my dresser drawer. I knew even then that part of me was pushing her away to make it easier for myself when she was gone.

I left home after high school graduation to study abroad in Spain. I was eighteen and desperate to get away. Still, I returned home for Christmas six months later to find my mother's hair grown thin and her right arm bloated and white, a new tumor blocking the blood flow through her body. Within three months, she would be dead.

Her death became the great smoldering divide of my life. I came to see cancer as a kind of possession in itself: an evil that invades and corrodes the body, corrupting it from within. Even years later, when I read Susan Sontag and tried my best to heed her warnings, I still clung tightly to my metaphor. It made sense to me. I no longer feared being possessed by the devil, but I feared this new kind of invasion, one that no priest could save me from. I came to see myself as precancerous, simply biding my time until my rogue cells began to relentlessly divide. I awaited this with a kind of mournful softness, in the secret hope that it would, at last, bring me close to my mother again.

•

When I watch *The Exorcist* now, I think about all of the things my mother didn't tell me about the film. Gore, profanity, and blood-chilling horror aside, *The Exorcist*, when you really get down to it, is just a story about a mother and a daughter.

In its early scenes, *The Exorcist* is careful to depict the intense love that exists between Chris and Regan. Regan steals food off the kitchen table and Chris chases after her, wrestling her to the ground in a delirious fit of giggles. Chris and Regan joke and laugh in the basement, idly chatting about horses and board games and papier-mâché. Chris tucks Regan in at night and whispers "I love you," the last thing Regan hears before she falls asleep.

These establishing scenes of intimacy and warmth make the proceeding horror—Regan stabbing herself with a crucifix,

shoving her mother's face into her bloody crotch, and growling, "Eat me, eat me," for example—even more shocking. The
film brilliantly dramatizes Chris and Regan's close emotional
bond and then exaggerates the brutality of its eventual decline,
showing the ways deep love can quickly devolve into hate, how
those things can, and often do, exist at the exact same time.

Beyond whatever political and social anxieties it seemed to
express in 1973, *The Exorcist* hits upon a primal fear: The
daughter will reject and loathe the mother, the mother will
resent and fear the daughter. It is worth emphasizing that
Blatty named his possessed child Regan after one of *King
Lear*'s famously thankless daughters. The mother-daughter
relationship is inevitably shaped by the looming specter of
abandonment and loss. As Adrienne Rich says, "The loss of
daughter to the mother, mother to the daughter, is the essential
female tragedy."

The relationship between Chris and Regan isn't the only
fraught parent-child bond in the film. Father Karras also suffers guilt from the recent death of his sick mother, who eerily
appears to him in dreams and during Regan's exorcism. Yet,
unlike this relationship, which is shallow and ultimately
doomed, Chris and Regan's bond holds within it the possibility for redemption, of loss regained.

At the end of the film, there lies the other promise of mothers and daughters, a promise so often left unfulfilled: The
daughter, waking up from a long and frightful dream, crawls
into a dusty corner of her room and calls out for her mother.
Her mother, hesitant at first, runs to and envelopes her daughter in her arms, everything forgiven.

•

I finally saw *The Exorcist* in its entirety five years after my
mother died, on a drizzly Friday night in October. I was

twenty-three and seeing a lot of movies by myself in those days. Almost every night, I'd smoke a joint and walk miles in the dark to the nearest theater in town where I could sit in front of a screen for hours and forget the world around me. That night, I rode my bike to the Academy, a second-run theater in Southeast Portland that was showing their original 1973 print of *The Exorcist* as part of a Halloween marathon. Though the theater was less than half full, a middle-aged man in a baseball cap sat in the seat directly in front of me. He turned to me, a condescending smile on his face.

"You know this is a very scary movie," he said. "Don't you?"

I smiled politely and nodded.

The theater was cold, and I left my heavy jacket on for the length of the film. I spent the entire time bracing myself for the spider-walk scene that never came. Somehow this felt right— I was seeing the version my mother had first seen all those decades ago. I watched the film from start to finish, not disturbed or traumatized, but enthralled. My eyes welled up during the final exorcism scene, in that moment when the mother and the daughter hold each other in their arms.

After that night, I watched *The Exorcist* obsessively. It no longer terrified me. It fascinated me. I came to see the film as a way to connect with my mother and all the different versions of her I never knew. I accepted the film and all its problems as part of me, probably a larger part of me than it was of her, and I didn't mind. Watching it became a way of calling her forth, of keeping her close.

Mother, Mother, I would silently pray with each passing frame. *If you are there, come.*

EXCAVATION

A bright yellow sun hanging in a blood-red sky. The silhouette of ancient city walls looming on the heat-warped horizon. Men thrusting pickaxes into crumbling earth, stirring up thick clouds of dry dust. A young boy racing through the ruins with a message.

People tend to forget that this is how *The Exorcist* begins. The images of what happens to the possessed little girl inside that cloistered Georgetown house are almost powerful enough to eclipse the rest of the film's frames. Unless you watch the director's cut, which does in fact open with a brief shot of the famed brick house on 3600 Prospect Street, *The Exorcist* begins not in the autumnal streets of Washington, DC, but in the city of Mosul in Northern Iraq.

The first thing we hear after the atonal strings that screech over the film's opening credits is the distorted echo of the Islamic call to prayer, firmly situating Western viewers in the vaguely threatening land of the Other. Father Merrin, a Catholic priest and seasoned exorcist, is in Mosul on an archeology dig, sifting through the Mesopotamian ruins of Nineveh in search of ancient artifacts.

Perhaps not surprisingly, *The Exorcist*'s Mosul sequence indulges in some fairly unabashed Orientalism: Bearded men hock tea in bustling markets, old women haunt twisting streets in black robes, camels crest the top of almost every distant hill. In the novel, Father Merrin meets with the curator of antiquities and notices, quite unnecessarily, "a speck of boiled chickpea nestled in a corner of the Arab's mouth." The film stock itself seems to speed up in these early scenes; the characters move about at a frantic, almost inhuman pace. Watching it, one feels disjointed, dizzy. This feverish open brings to mind *Casablanca*'s Morocco: a Hollywood version of a foreign land. Even if *The Exorcist*'s Mosul sequence was indeed filmed on location in Iraq, it is oddly set-like.

Father Merrin is digging through the dusty ruins of Nineveh when a young boy runs through the site to tell him there's been a discovery. "Small pieces," the boy explains. Father Merrin follows him to a trench at the base of the mound, where another archeologist shows the priest a Christian medal engraved with the image of St. Joseph.

"This is strange," Father Merrin remarks in Arabic, though a more literal translation might be: "Why is this here?"

Merrin's eyes are then drawn to a crumbling hole in the sediment. He reaches inside and pulls out another dirt-caked artifact: a small statue of Pazuzu, the ancient king of the wind demons. In Mesopotamian mythology, Pazuzu was an essential God, yet feared. He was known to bring famine, drought, and locusts but also to protect mankind from the malevolent demigoddess, Lamashtu, who haunted pregnant women and drank the blood of their children. She is associated with disturbing sleep, bringing nightmares, and spreading disease and death.

Jarred by the discovery at the site, Father Merrin stumbles back to town. He wanders about the streets of Mosul in his archeologist garb—khakis, olive drab button-up, sunhat—looking weak and confused. One too many exorcisms have sent him over the edge, and he pops mysterious white pills to stop the nearly constant shaking in his hands. Though Swedish actor Max von Sydow was only forty-three when he took the role of Lankester Merrin, pioneering makeup artist Dick Smith made him appear decades older: sagging eyes, cracked lips, crepe paper-thin skin. Sydow trembles and slumps, transforming into a man almost broken by the things he has seen. In the novel, Blatty describes the way the devil follows Merrin like a shadow: "And yes he was here, the air was thick with him, that Other who ravaged his dreams."

Eventually, Merrin finds his way back to the ruins. A shadow falls across his path and he looks up to find a giant statue in the desert, sprouted seemingly out of nowhere. It depicts a menacing, winged man-beast with the head of a lion, the tail of a scorpion, and a massive, snake-wrapped hard-on. The statue stops Merrin in his tracks. Pazuzu once again. Two dogs snarl and fight in the distance. Strings screech as Merrin stares up in horror, a celibate Catholic priest facing off with an evil, erect monster of the East.

These visual and aural motifs occur throughout the rest of the film. Audiences are meant to understand then that the medal, the statues, and the priest are somehow connected with the possession of Regan MacNeil before it has even begun. Perhaps this is the moment when the demon slips into Regan's body while she sleeps.

Father Merrin traveled to Nineveh to dig his way out of the horror that haunts him. Dig deep enough, and he might find salvation. As Merrin faces off with Pazuzu in the blazing sun, it is clear he will have to go deeper to find the resolution he seeks. He will exorcise the devil one more time before he can at last be free.

•

I believe that a single film, or even just a few frames of a single film, can enthrall, disturb, and perplex an individual for their entire life. It happened to my mother, and it happened to me. Maybe it has happened to you too.

I was deeply captivated by the 2012 documentary film *Room 237*—about people who fanatically watch Stanley Kubrick's *The Shining* in search of the hidden meaning that lurks within—not because I was necessarily swayed by the in-depth breakdown of the film's phallic imagery or by its many professed theories connecting *The Shining* to the Native American genocide and the moon landing, but more so because I can relate to the all-consuming force of the interviewees' obsession, the compulsive watching and rewatching of a film until it becomes part of you, mining every scene for undiscovered secrets and surprises until you convince yourself that buried deep somewhere within each frame is an answer, even if it is just the answer to the question of why this film holds such power over you. *Room 237* is evidence that anyone can watch a film and discover something new. It is also a sobering reminder that this type of creative, ultra-close analysis can be dangerous, turning a film into fodder for quasi–conspiracy theorists who dissect each frame for meanings that only serve to confirm their existing beliefs.

Interestingly, Warner Bros. approached Kubrick to direct *The Exorcist* before Friedkin signed on. The studio also approached Mike Nichols, who passed because he didn't want the fate of the film resting in the hands of a child actor; Peter Bogdanovich, who passed because he was pursuing other projects at the time; and Arthur Penn, who passed because he was busy teaching at Yale. Kubrick declined because he was too deeply involved in his failing Napoleon project, and because the studios wouldn't let him produce, which, as any Kubrick fan knows, was almost certainly a deal breaker. It would be seven years before Kubrick's first real foray into horror, but perhaps the success of *The Exorcist* showed him that horror was a genre ready-made for the kind of visual excess, psychological intensity, and sly social commentary that he strove for with every film.

In his book *Zona*, a brilliant and at times suffocatingly close reading of Tarkovsky's *Stalker*, Geoff Dyer writes, "The forgetting and not noticing is an authentic and integral part of watching any film—and this book is an account of watching, remembering, misremembering, and forgetting; it is not the record of a dissection." It is that process of rediscovery, of remembering what you have misremembered, that makes rewatching a film such a profound delight. Just as we reexamine our own lives, we rewatch films in order to unearth the things we have missed or forgotten, to sift through the layers of meaning that accumulate with time, and to notice how our understanding and appreciation of an immutable cinematic artifact changes as we do. It's comforting, in its own way, to know that while our own memories might shift and fade, the movies we love remain exactly the same.

There are, of course, certain movies we rewatch simply to revisit the sheer pleasure they bring us. For me, it's mostly the comedies I watched constantly as a child and teen. These films are always exactly as I remember them, and I'm comforted by their lasting pleasures. I can recite almost every line from *Zoolander*, and I still think of it every time I hear Wham! or read the word *eulogy*. *Mrs. Doubtfire* is the same every time Robin Williams emerges from the refrigerator with his face covered in whipped cream, and I still laugh the way I always have when he is cooking dinner and extinguishes the flames on his fake chest using the lids of two pans. I've watched these films so many times that their every frame and line are embedded in my psyche, whereas no matter how many times I watch *The Exorcist*, I always get scenes out of order or misremember certain lines. *Does Regan punch the hypnotist in the balls before or after she masturbates with the crucifix? How many times does Father Karras visit Regan before she projectile vomits on his face?* I'm always making new connections and discoveries, always writing things down and then returning to the film later to make sure I got them right. Simply put, it is a different film every time I watch it, and yet it feels concrete and linear and legible in a way that my own life so often does not. This is the promise of the return viewing: that one day, the thing that has eluded and mystified me for years will be within my control, and I'll be released from it, unpossessed.

As Robin Wood writes in "An Introduction to the American Horror Film," perhaps the first critical text to take horror seriously as a genre, "One might say that the true subject of the horror genre is the struggle for recognition of all that our civilization represses or oppresses." Wood gets at the sheer pleasure and necessity of film criticism, the importance of rewatching films and thinking deeply about them. You watch a horror film not only to search for what is buried deep within its frames but also to search for what is buried deep within the culture that the film reflects. We watch and rewatch movies to discover what they tell us about ourselves and the world around us, and maybe even to free ourselves in the process.

•

Its status as a horror film tends to sideline *The Exorcist* when naming the great films of the 1970s. Surely *The Godfather I* and *II, Taxi Driver, Nashville, Chinatown, Annie Hall,* and *Dog Day Afternoon* get quicker and more exuberant praise. Incest, child prostitution, and grisly murder are apparently palatable additions to the cinematic canon; demonic possession and crucifix masturbation decidedly are not. Nonetheless, *The Exorcist* is a groundbreaking hallmark of 1970s filmmaking, a film that epitomizes everything that made the decade so thrilling, iconic, and, ultimately, doomed.

The films associated with New Hollywood tend to evoke words like *bold, gritty,* and *masterful.* Also, depending on who you're talking to, *misogynistic, violent,* and *big-headed.* Whatever you have to say about the whiteness, the maleness, and the self-importance of 1970s filmmaking, it was undeniably a decade that changed the history of cinema forever.

The rise and fall of New Hollywood has been much mythologized, which is not surprising considering the racial and gender demographics of its most famous auteurs. Usually, when praising New Hollywood, people start at the beginning of the 1960s, when Hollywood was in crisis mode. Movie attendance was at an all-time low as rising television ownership made inroads against traditional theatergoing. Nearly 90 percent of American households owned televisions, and ploys like rocking-chair movie seats, Cinerama, or complimentary pieces of dinnerware with the purchase of every ticket weren't enough to coax families off their couches and back to the theaters. The old studios, ruled by out-of-touch peons like Adolph Zukor and Louis B. Mayer, were crumbling, and the female-centric star system that once drew audiences to the movies had lost its magnetic pull.

Seeing an opening, a trove of hungry white male directors seized on the fissures of the old system and forced their way in, directing a wave of dark, complex, and often groundbreaking mainstream films like nothing American audiences had seen in years. Under this new crop of directors—Coppola, Scorsese, Altman, Spielberg, Bogdanovich, Friedkin—the 1970s became a "director's decade," or, as Molly Haskell calls it in *From Reverence to Rape,* an era of "directorial demigoddery." These artists, and artists they insisted they were, embraced meandering, fragmented narratives that rejected contemporary Hollywood's pat morals and happy endings. With the death of the Motion Picture Production Code and gradually eroding taboos around sexuality and perceived vulgarity, these filmmakers were free to glorify violence, use foul language, display drug use, show nudity (female nudity, of course), and, for the first time in the history of cinema, starting with Robert Altman's *M*A*S*H* in 1970, openly ridicule a belief in God. After the 1970s, husbands and wives in the movies would no longer go to sleep in separate twin beds. More filmmakers and moviegoers embraced the ethic of Arthur Penn, who said of his film *Bonnie and Clyde,* "We're in the Vietnam War. This film cannot be immaculate and sanitized and bang-bang. It's fucking bloody."

The grand artistic ambitions and thrilling boldness of these directors were often engulfed, not surprisingly, by excess, egos, and drugs. In William Friedkin's words, "Arrogance and pussy were the double pronged temptresses for guys in our position. We all thought that we were the center of the universe and everything revolved around our problems, our needs, our ambitions." At the beginning of the decade, movies rarely cost more than $8 million to produce. By mid-decade, they were costing upwards of $30 million. Films routinely went over budget, over schedule, and over the top. For example, Coppola wanted to make a ten-hour, 3D version of Goethe's *Elective Affinities.* The eccentricities of the New Hollywood elite were almost as famous as their films. You might know the stories: The entire cast and crew of *Easy Rider* getting so baked that they forgot to film one of the most important scenes, directors carefully calibrating the amount of drugs to give Jack Nicholson before shooting each scene, Dennis Hopper chasing his wife with a gun, producers keeping bowls of weed on their office tables, and a never-ending flow of beautiful women floating in and out of certain director's hot tubs, often while their wives waited patiently upstairs.

As egos and budgets grew, so did audiences. Peter Biskind writes in *Easy Riders, Raging Bulls,* "Film was no less than a secular religion." By 1974 film grosses were higher than their postwar boom. After a decades-long plateau, people went to the movies again, talked about the movies again, and cared about the movies again. This most American of industries had been boldly and problematically reborn.

Though still mostly corralled within the confines of what Robin Wood calls "the disreputable genre," the 1970s also marked the moment, helped along by hits like *Psycho* in 1960 and *Rosemary's Baby* in 1968, when actors and directors could take on the horror genre without putting the final nail in the coffin of their artistic careers. Ruth Gordon won the 1969 Academy Award for Best Supporting Actress for her role as the nosey, Satan-worshipping neighbor in *Rosemary's Baby*. *The Exorcist* was the first horror film to be nominated for Best Picture at the Academy Awards, and it remained the highest-grossing horror film of all time until the *IT* remake knocked it to second place in 2017. From Brian De Palma to Jordan Peele, generations of auteurs can hold up *The Exorcist* as evidence of the awesome power a mainstream horror film can wield when done right.

•

William Peter Blatty published his best-selling novel *The Exorcist* in 1971 after spending several years languishing in Hollywood and writing a series of comedic screenplays with punctuation marks in the title. See: *John Goldfarb, Please Come Home!* and *What Did You Do in the War, Daddy?* Blatty's employment history up to that point had been sporadic and picaresque. He'd worked as a vacuum cleaner salesman, a beer truck driver, and a United Airlines ticket agent. As a young adult, he spent many years in Washington, DC, where

The Exorcist is set, earning a bachelor's degree in English from Georgetown University and a master's degree from George Washington University. While at Georgetown, he briefly considered joining the priesthood as a Jesuit, and he would later say that writing *The Exorcist* was his way of atoning for his failed career as a seminarian. Instead, he did a stint in the US Air Force and eventually became head of the policy branch at their Psychological Warfare Division. Later, he worked for the US Information Agency in Beirut. Throughout, he dreamt of becoming an actor, only abandoning the dream when he was rejected for the role of Moses in Cecil B. DeMille's *The Ten Commandments* on account of his piercing blue eyes. Eventually, in 1961, he won $10,000 on the Groucho Marx–hosted quiz show, *You Bet Your Life,* which allowed him to quit working and dedicate himself to writing off-the-wall comedies and spy spoofs.

It wasn't until 1969 that Blatty decided to start working on *The Exorcist,* using as inspiration an old *Washington Post* article about the possession of a young boy named Robbie Mannheim in Mount Rainer, Maryland. Blatty had read the article twenty years before, when he was a junior at Georgetown. The headline: "Priest Faces Mt. Rainer Boy Reportedly Held in Devil's Grip." As Blatty recounts in his book *If There Were Demons Then Perhaps There Were Angels,* the article struck him as "tangible evidence of transcendence" and may have sparked his fleeting desire to become a priest. Blatty writes, "If there were demons then there were angels and probably a God and life everlasting." Though the case both haunted and inspired him for decades, it took twenty years and many career shifts before he realized it was "a worthy subject for a novel."

The Robbie Mannheim possession began in January 1949 on 3210 Bunker Hill Road, when Robbie's parents heard scratching and dripping noises coming from the attic. Just as Chris MacNeil does in *The Exorcist*, they dismissed it as rats and went on with their lives. However, things got notably worse when Robbie's aunt Harriet, a self-proclaimed medium who had previously taught Robbie to use a ouija board, died in St. Louis. Robbie began using foul and sacrilegious language, often centered around sexual relations between priests and nuns. Mattresses defied the laws of physics. Robbie's room seethed with a strange and unbearable odor. Thumps and roars echoed through the house without any discernable source. Armchairs raced across the room as if possessed themselves. Robbie became suddenly and inexplicably fluent in Latin.

Eventually, the parents sent Robbie off to a Lutheran minister who concluded that the case was way past his pay grade. "You have to see a Catholic priest," he reportedly said. "The Catholics know about things like this." After a failed exorcism at the Jesuit run Georgetown Hospital, during which Robbie reportedly attacked Father Albert Hughes with a broken bedspring, an experienced exorcist named Father William Bowdern arrived on the scene with two assistants, Father Bishop and Father Halloran, and the standard exorcism toolkit: a Bible, some holy water, and a defined set of prayers and incantations to recite over the child's writhing body.

During the exorcism, words like *Hell* and *Spite* routinely formed on Robbie's skin, as if etched there from the inside, an eerie, visceral torture that also happens to Regan MacNeil in *The Exorcist*. Once, his parents even found the word *Exit* carved onto his stomach, accompanied by two arrows pointing down past his underwear. At one point, Robbie's fingers appeared to be webbed. In *If There Were Demons Then Perhaps There Were Angels*, Blatty cites a report "that the exorcist and his assistants were forced to wear rubber wind-jammer suits, for the boy, in his fits, displayed a prodigious ability to urinate endlessly, accurately, and over great distances, with the exorcists as his target." Finally, on the eighteenth of April, after nearly two months of work, Father Bowdern cried out, "In the name of the Father, Son, and the Holy Spirit, I cast thee out," successfully purging Satan from Robbie's body.

Robbie reportedly had no memory of the horrific events, including any recall for Latin. Besides the article in the *Washington Post,* the Mannheims kept their son out of the spotlight, hoping that Robbie would go through his life without the glare of media attention, the trauma of knowing what he had lived through, or the recurrence of any demonic visits. When Blatty approached the Catholic Church years later for a case history of the possession, both the archbishop and Robbie's parents denied him permission. Blatty then embarked upon a rigorous period of research, consulting theologians, psychiatrists, ethnologists, and philosophers. Though the possessed child remained a boy in earlier drafts of the novel, Blatty, hoping to put a little distance between his story and the Mannheim's, eventually made the fortuitous decision to change Robbie to Regan. Eventually, after numerous rejections, skepticism from many—from his agent to his dentist—and a slightly delirious dinner party pitch to an editor at Bantam Press, Blatty found a willing publisher and finished writing *The Exorcist* in the summer of 1970.

Despite Blatty's confidence in the material, *The Exorcist* wasn't a success upon its initial publication. *The Exorcist* likely would have vanished into obscurity if it weren't for a last-minute cancellation on the *Dick Cavett Show.* Desperate for someone to fill the spot, Cavett's people called Blatty. As luck would have it, the guest before Blatty, Robert Shaw, showed up drunk, and his interview was cut short, giving Blatty a solid forty-five minutes to talk about his novel of demonic possession. Within ten days of his appearance on the show, *The Exorcist* was number four on the *New York Times* Best Sellers list.

Blatty signed a contract with Warner Bros. as the film's screenwriter and producer. He has said of his decision to adapt the book, "I thought it was impossible. And immediately agreed to do it." But adapting his beloved novel for the screen was no easy task. To borrow Blatty's own words, "Film is an industry in which writers are either broken or wind up senselessly murdering strangers in the streets." Blatty's original screenplay was a whopping 225 pages long, which would have amounted to about a four-hour runtime. It wasn't until William Friedkin, the young hotshot director of *The French Connection*, signed on as director that the script was pruned to an appropriate (and award-winning) length. Apparently, Friedkin simply circled large chunks of the novel he wanted turned into scenes and told Blatty to excise the rest. It was this type of directness that Blatty had valued in Friedkin long before they teamed up for *The Exorcist*. The two had tried to work on another project together before, and Blatty, a Lebanese Catholic, fondly remembered the Jewish Friedkin's refreshing honesty about a scene in Blatty's screenplay that he declared "the worst piece of shit I've read in my life."

Friedkin has said that "a good part of my motivation" for taking on *The Exorcist* was to "make a better film than Francis." Though he is often overshadowed by Coppola and the decade's other directorial greats, Friedkin shared their same radical vision, their same unfettered boldness and masculine bravado, their same zealous dedication in bringing their vision to reality with little regard for empathy or practicalities. A former documentary filmmaker, Friedkin was one of New Hollywood's "film brats," an auteur raised on a steady diet of French New Wave and postwar Japanese cinema who willingly eschewed common decency in order to bring his vision to life.

Friedkin was prone to ego trips and temper tantrums like many other New Hollywood directors. While filming *The Exorcist,* he sat in a cloth-backed chair with the words *An Oscar for the French Connection* stenciled on the back. Nicknamed "Wacky Willy," he was known for firing off guns on the set and playing tapes at high volume over the sound system: recordings of the *Psycho* soundtrack or the loud chirping of South American tree frogs. He also liked to slap his actors, a trick he apparently learned from John Ford. Perhaps most famously, he slapped Father William O'Malley, the real priest who played Father Dyer in *The Exorcist.* O'Malley was struggling through the scene in which Father Dyer delivers Father Karras his last rites at the foot of the famous staircase, still unable to nail it after the thirtieth take. In order to help stimulate the correct level of shock and emotion (and to wrap up what was proving to be a long and damp night shoot), Friedkin smacked O'Malley across the face. According to Friedkin, the following take is the one we see in the film. Friedkin maintains that after filming the scene, Father O'Malley thanked and embraced the director for helping him to reach the scene's emotional heart.

Though there were occasional disagreements throughout the filming of *The Exorcist,* tension between Blatty and Friedkin reached a fever pitch during the editing process, when Friedkin insisted on further cutting many of the scenes Blatty considered central to the film's message. Blatty felt that Friedkin's cut, though highly effective, lacked a clear spiritual center. He told Mark Kermode in 1998, "You proceeded from shock to shock without a clear purpose." And for Blatty, the purpose was clear. *The Exorcist,* by showing the presence of evil in the world, was supposed to confirm the presence of God.

Friedkin told Kermode that he wanted the final cut to be "leaner and meaner, to keep the story moving forward."

While editing, he "felt like the magician who wanted to get off stage as fast as possible, before the audience saw through the tricks." Friedkin was opposed to Blatty's arguably heavy-handed approach to the film's meaning, and he excised any moments in the film that seemed designed to uplift or convert. This rift between the writer and the director would remain unresolved for decades.

•

When talking with someone about *The Exorcist*, it might be a good idea to stop and ask, "Well, which one?" Several different versions of *The Exorcist* have been released over the years, lending the film a mysterious and endlessly mutable quality, as if "the real *Exorcist*" is forever waiting to be discovered in the vaults at Warner Bros. Especially dedicated viewers may feel that their understanding of it will never be comprehensive or complete. This, I'm sure, is partly why I'm always wrongly recalling scenes or remembering them out of order. Perhaps I feel like I am watching a different movie every time because in some cases I actually am.

There is, of course, the original 1973 version, which my mother saw when she snuck off to watch the film in Canby that Christmas. Then there are the censored TV versions, edited to include far less profane language, obscenity, and gore. Instead of bringing Mercedes McCambridge back to redub the demon's lines, Friedkin did the redubbing himself, switching out the line "Your mother sucks cocks in hell" for "Your mother still rots in hell!" The "Shove it up your ass, you f****t" line was redubbed without the *ass*, but the *f****t* still rang out loud and clear (this was 1980.) Ellen Burstyn also came back into the studio to redub a few of Chris's lines, swapping "Jesus Christ!" out for "Judas Priest!" The scene of

Regan stabbing herself in the vagina with a crucifix was, not surprisingly, also cut.

Twenty-five years after the film's premiere, Friedkin and Blatty began editing the film for an anniversary rerelease, titled somewhat cheekily *The Exorcist: The Version You've Never Seen*. Friedkin agreed to reexamine the film and to consider putting in the missing scenes Blatty had so mourned losing in the 1973 cut. Throughout the years, Blatty maintained that a positive spiritual message remained buried in the film's outtakes. Only through returning to *The Exorcist* archives, which were then spread out between the Warner Bros. vaults, a lot in Burbank, and an old salt mine in Kansas where the negatives were stored, could the true film be unearthed.

The 25th Anniversary Special Edition version includes the infamous spider-walk shot, additional scenes of Regan's doctor visits, and a conversation between Father Karras and Father Merrin on the staircase about the meaning of Regan's possession that Blatty considered to be the key to the film. Other scenes were excised or shortened, and more subliminal images were added. The original ending was extended. The film was also remastered using new technology, building upon the film's already eerie soundscape. Though he perhaps entered into the reedit begrudgingly, Friedkin admitted he liked what the new technology allowed him to do. It gave him the freedom, he said, "to imply the presence of the demon in places that are totally unexpected."

After spending so much time digging through the outtakes, Friedkin also admitted that he finally understood what Blatty had wanted to do with the picture. Friedkin said to Mark Kermode in 1998, "Viewing both versions now, I can see the old version is a colder film, more dyspeptic and abstract, more like a piece of contemporary music than a classical piece. This new version is much warmer. And, I think, much better." Blatty, too, was satisfied with the release. This is why calling the 25th Anniversary Special Edition a "director's cut" is a misnomer. Really, it is the director resurrecting the writer's original vision.

All movies, of course, are an assemblage of fragments miraculously spliced together to form something coherent. Filmmaking is a mad attempt to tell a story out of a disjointed scramble of image and sound, to form a narrative out of the visual chaos tapped from reality. There are likely hundreds of different possible versions for each film made, some versions much worse than the masterpiece that eventually graces the screens, some arguably superior. From the bits and pieces that had lingered unseen for a quarter century, Friedkin and Blatty reassembled a version of the film that felt better, truer. Blatty, at last, was content. He told Mark Kermode, "After all this time I finally feel like the movie does what I wanted it to do—and what I always thought the book did too. To excite the audience, but also to inspire in them a sense of the reality of transcendence, to startle them with a credible confrontation with the forces of the supernatural, and ultimately, to leave them with the impression that it would all be all right in the end."

This is perhaps the most surprising aspect of Blatty's vision. His intention for *The Exorcist* was not to frighten or disturb or scare into devotional submission. He wanted his film to comfort.

Linda Blair advanced a similar interpretation of the film in a later interview with Mark Kermode. "There are different ways of interpreting the film," she said, "Bill Blatty probably has his own version, and Friedkin has his. But for me, it says that we're only on this planet for a very short time, and we can walk in a good or a bad light. . . . I just wish that the film had affected people in a more positive way, to make them follow a more spiritual path."

The Exorcist can be interpreted as a reflection of the male fear of the maturing female body, an exploration of the sexual repression inherent to the American nuclear family, a warning against the diminishing presence of religion in the United States, or a symbol for the backlash against a steadily liberalizing American culture. You can say it is a reaction against feminism, abortion, single parenthood, hippies, atheism, youth culture, the civil rights movement, puberty, or Hollywood itself. I once found myself forming an in-depth, nuanced argument that *The Exorcist* foretold the precipitous rise of neoliberalism and the religious right in the 1980s (Regan = Reagan?!) There's a lengthy YouTube video dissecting *The Exorcist* as a graphic tale of child abuse. Some argue that the film is actually about the latent homosexual desire shared between the two priests, Father Merrin and Father Karras. When Karras finally summons the devil out of Regan's body at the end of the film, he cries "Leave the girl and take me! Take me! Come into me!" When the devil does, Karras throws himself out the window, simultaneously crushing and fulfilling his repressed homosexuality.

It seems to me that *The Exorcist* is one of those films that explicitly asks its viewers to take up the task of interpreting. It is, in part, a movie about movies. In fact, film making, film fandom, and film criticism play a surprisingly large part in *The Exorcist*.

Chris MacNeil, the mother of the possessed girl Regan, is a famous actress on location in DC to film *Crash Course*, a movie about campus protests that she describes as "the Walt Disney version of the Ho Chi Minh story." Blatty claims to have modeled Chris after his good friend and neighbor Shirley MacLaine, who eventually went on to star in the rival picture *The Possession of Joel Delaney*. One of the film's early scenes is a dynamic set piece where crowds of spectators, Father Karras included, gather around the Georgetown campus to watch the *Crash Course* film crew in action. A minor though important character in *The Exorcist* is the booze-guzzling film director Burke Dennings, who dies in a freak accident involving a bedroom window and a steep flight of stairs. It is implied, though never explicitly confirmed, that Regan killed him. What's more, the lead detective on the case is an unabashed cinephile named Lieutenant Kinderman. During his investigation, Kinderman tracks down Father Karras to ask if the priest has noticed any unusual activity among the seminarians. He ends their interview by inviting Karras to the movies with him (he gets discounted passes at the local theaters).

"I like to talk film," Kinderman says. "Discuss. Critique."

Karras declines the offer but laughs when Kinderman compares him to the actor Sal Mineo.

Later, Kinderman visits Chris to interview her and investigate the scene of the potential crime. He gushes that he saw her film *Angel* six times and asks for an autograph for his niece, later sheepishly admitting that the autograph was really for him. The last scene in the reedited version of the film is Kinderman inviting Father Dyer to see *Wuthering Heights* with him. Though they've both already seen the movie, they decide it's worth the rewatch.

In fact, the very last line in *The Exorcist* was intended to be about movies. It was not included in either cut of the film because the sound quality was too poor, but you can find it online. As Dyer and Kinderman walk away from the house on 3600 Prospect Street, Kinderman quotes *Casablanca*: "I think this is the beginning of a beautiful friendship." Dyer laughs and tells Kinderman that he looks a bit like Humphrey Bogart. Fade to black.

•

Films like *The Exorcist* compel viewers to rewatch and rediscover them, to dig about for the countless hidden clues the filmmakers left within, whether or not they were intentional. Friedkin and Blatty understood the power of cinema, and *The Exorcist* seems to be saying that if you watch the film, or any good film for that matter, with enough attention and care, you'll be amazed by the meaning and terror you can excavate from its frames.

One of the overarching theories of *Room 237* holds that *The Shining* is really about the manifold historical atrocities that we have largely repressed and ignored—Native American genocide, the Holocaust, etc.—but that will eventually force their way to the surface and spill forth into our consciousness, an idea perfectly encapsulated by the unforgettable image of blood pouring out of the Overlook Hotel's half-shut elevator doors. The interviewees find the clues to this interpretation everywhere, in cans of Calumet baking powder and in Jack's Adler typewriter. The director of the documentary eventually asks one of *The Shining*–obsessed interviewees why exactly Stanley Kubrick decided to make his horror classic so damn complicated and opaque.

"It's a way of opening doors from a hermetically sealed reality, into possibilities," the interviewee responds. "And it's also a way of trapping someone like me, who goes looking for clues and keeps finding them."

He chuckles and then, as if to exonerate Kubrick, adds, "But there are escape routes. He puts escape routes into his maze, into his trap. There are ways of getting out of it."

THE LOUD SILENCE

One of the many interlocking reasons that *The Exorcist* so shocked and unsettled audiences in the early 1970s was its rumored use of subliminal images. Viewers left the theater terrified that something ancient and evil had been beamed into their minds without their consent. Wilson Bryan Key's popular book *Subliminal Seduction* had been released that same year, direly warning readers, "Every person reading this book has been victimized and manipulated by the use of subliminal stimuli directed into his unconscious mind by the mass merchandisers of media." The book's front cover depicts a dripping glass of gin, a lemon peel floating among the ice, and above it, the question *Are you being sexually aroused by this picture?* The back cover lists the various ways *Subliminal Seduction* will help the average American defend themselves against "media rape." The takeaway, basically, is that all types of perverse and insidious messages, usually sexual in nature, are being injected into fragile subconscious minds via sounds and images that exist beneath the threshold of conscious perception.

Subliminal Seduction is a weirdly puritanical text in that Key attempts to warn readers about the dangerous pornographic content hidden in advertising while at the same time encouraging readers to scour every commercial, magazine ad, and billboard for that same dangerous pornographic content. The man who was so affronted by potential penis shapes in cigarette ads sure spent a lot of time looking for penis shapes in cigarette ads. Still, *Subliminal Seduction*'s fierce anticorporate sentiment feels oddly ahead of its time, as do apocalyptic lines like this: "In a world such as this one, straining from population growth and resource depletion, the ability to differentiate between illusion and reality will soon become an even greater necessity to survival." To a fragmented and vulnerable American public, one that was becoming increasingly skeptical of once-trusted institutions like advertising, newspapers, and indeed the government, Key's arguments had power. *Subliminal Seduction* taught readers that not even the private world of the individual mind was safe from capitalist invasion. A year after the book hit shelves, the FCC released an official statement warning consumers about subliminal messaging in the media.

Of course, subliminal messages, or as Key calls them, "embeds," weren't anything new. Some say they date all the way back to the fifth century BC, when the Greeks first began using persuasive linguistic tools to influence those around them. The United States government introduced them as early as 1943, when the words *BUY BONDS* briefly flashed on screen during an animated Donald Duck short. The public had first become aware of subliminal images as we understand them now a couple of decades before Key's book was published, after the famous 1956 Vicary experiment in which the words *Drink Coca-Cola* and *Hungry? Eat Popcorn* were flashed on a theater screen in Fort Lee, New Jersey, for 1/3000th of a second during a six-week run of the film *Picnic*. James Vicary concluded that these subliminal projections led to a marked increase in drink and snack sales throughout the region, though his data was later proven to be falsified. Vance

Packard's book *The Hidden Persuaders,* a precursor to *Subliminal Seduction,* was released a year later, exposing the techniques used by politicians and advertisers to manipulate and perhaps even to control the minds of the populace. Texas congressman James Wright even sponsored a bill forbidding the use of any device "designed to advertise a product or indoctrinate the public by means of making an impression on the subconscious mind."

But the frenzy about the use of subliminal messages in *The Exorcist* felt different. The fact that a mainstream Hollywood film was using this provocative technique, not just some soulless corporation trying to make a profit or a corrupt politician trying to snag a vote, scared some people more than the film itself. It begged the question: If the subliminal messages weren't there to sell anything, then why exactly were they there?

•

William Friedkin was inspired to use subliminal images in *The Exorcist* after seeing Alain Resnais's Holocaust documentary *Night and Fog,* in which peaceful shots of a now-abandoned German concentration camp are jarringly intercut with black-and-white footage of the corpses that were once piled on the grounds. "That seemed really profound to me when I first saw it," he said, "and that was my influence for the subliminal shots in *The Exorcist.* All of them were there to produce an effect like memory."

By my count, at least nine subliminal images appear in the 2000 rerelease of *The Exorcist.* We see the first at 0:31:29, as Regan is undergoing one of her many medical examinations. As she leans back on the examination table, a pale white face emerges from the shadows bearing sharp, rotting teeth. Beneath its wide eyes hang deep, red bags. The image is sometimes referred to as "the death mask." Some viewers have suggested that this is the face of Father Karras done up in creepy makeup, but Friedkin has said it is actually a still from a makeup test with Eileen Dietz, Linda Blair's body double.

The demon face appears again at 0:45:01 during an unsettling dream sequence in which Father Karras encounters his dead mother in the middle of a busy New York City thoroughfare. As if we have returned to the film's opening in Iraq, we also see brief shots of a falling medallion, a clock, dogs fighting in the sand, and the statue of Pazuzu.

At 0:56:03, when Chris is walking through the kitchen at 3600 Prospect Street, the lights flicker, and the demon face flashes on screen once again. Ten seconds later, as Chris reaches to open the door to Regan's bedroom, we see a close-up of Pazuzu's face. When Chris leaves the bedroom at 0:56:56, the full image of Pazuzu pulses in the shadows.

We see the demon face again at the one-hour mark, when Regan is undergoing hypnosis. The camera zooms up on her face and, for a quick flash, we see the image of a demonic face superimposed over hers.

A cluster of subliminal images also arises during the final exorcism sequence. At 1:43:13, as the lights blink on and off and Regan's possessed head whips wildly from side to side, the demonic face blazes onscreen over hers. At 1:45:23, Regan's head does another 360 and the demon face appears once again. And at 1:56:23, as the exorcism reaches its climax, Father Karras cries out to the devil: "Enter me! Enter me!" The devil obeys, and as Karras turns to the window, we see the ghostly image of his dead mother. The faint trace of her transparent face hovers over the curtains through which Karras will, seconds later, jump to his death.

Key's 1976 follow-up to *Subliminal Seduction*, *Media Sexploi-*

tation, devoted an entire chapter to *The Exorcist* called "*The Exorcist* Massage Parlor." Like *Subliminal Seduction,* the cover of *Media Sexploitation* features a provocative subtitle: *You Are Being Sexually Manipulated at This Very Moment. Do You Know How?* Also like its predecessor, the book encourages readers to do a lot of hokey detective work, such as searching for the ominous word *SEX* in the shadows of various commercial images, including an ad for Ritz crackers and a photograph of a Vietnamese woman featured in the *New York Times.*

Key applies this same level of bizarre scrutiny to *The Exorcist,* acknowledging the presence of several of the aforementioned subliminal images but also suggesting a few more that may or may not exist: phallic shadows cast by the posts on Regan's bed, a candle "ejaculating" a burst of flame as Chris searches for rats in the attic, and, most absurdly, the word *PIG* supposedly appearing on the staircase throughout the film. As far as I can tell, this last claim is pure invention, a fairly hysterical reference to both the Manson murders and the growing antipolice sentiment prevalent among Black and leftist communities at the time. Apparently for Key, the only thing more dangerous than a dick flashing on the screen was disrespect for the police.

In addition to the film's imagery, Key was keenly disturbed by *The Exorcist*'s Oscar-winning sound design. Music and sound are indeed crucial parts of *The Exorcist*'s horror, though not necessarily in the way you might expect. Many people have come to associate the film with its emblematic musical motif, "The Tubular Bells," by the English multi-instrumentalist Mike Oldfield. Originally, Bernard Herrmann was enlisted to compose the film's score. Herrmann had regularly composed for Hitchcock films, and his pioneering use of electronic instruments (theremins, electronic organ, etc.) made him an obvious choice for the film. However, Herrmann watched an early cut of *The Exorcist* and, according to Friedkin, immediately called it a "piece of shit." He would consent to work on *The Exorcist* only if Friedkin agreed to leave the cut with Herrmann and essentially let the master do his work. Friedkin declined.

Next, the director consulted Lalo Schifrin, an Argentine-born composer perhaps most famous for the *Mission Impossible* score. Schifrin brought a hundred musicians into a soundstage and recorded a heavy brass and percussive number that Friedkin deemed "fucking Mexican marimba music." Schifrin subsequently called working with Friedkin "one of the most unpleasant experiences of my life." With a release date looming, Friedkin retreated to the music library at Warner Bros. and found a track off Oldfield's debut, the prog-rock inspired orchestral album *Tubular Bells*. He was immediately drawn to the album's chilling opening melody in A minor, which is really just a small part of an epic, forty-nine-minute masterpiece featuring a pipe organ, glockenspiel, tin whistle, timpani drum, and guitars recorded at half speed. Another version of the story goes that Friedkin was visiting the offices of Ahmet Ertegun, president of Atlantic Records, and simply picked a record from his collection, put it on the record player, and decided it was perfect.

Though *Tubular Bells* did not perform particularly well upon its initial release, after *The Exorcist,* it reached number one in the UK, Canada, and Australia, totaling $17 million in sales and helping to jumpstart the success of Virgin Records. Oldfield, who recorded the album at age nineteen and played almost all of the instruments himself, later admitted he was frightened of the film when it first came out and did not see it until ten years later.

Though Oldfield's iconic composition is widely considered an essential element of *The Exorcist*'s terror, in truth, it is played only twice in the film: when Chris is walking home from filming *Crash Course* on a blustery autumn day, and at the very end. Much of *The Exorcist*'s auditory tension is instead due to an eerie and nuanced soundscape that you may only notice if you are paying very close attention. Friedkin has admitted to inserting the barely discernable sounds of buzzing bees and industrial clanking to create an ominous, threatening mood throughout the film. In addition, he reduced normal sound levels so that audiences would have to unconsciously strain to hear the dialogue. What viewers may assume are frequent periods of silence are instead animated by low-frequency background hums that reach a crescendo and then slither off into nothingness. The not-silent silences are also frequently interrupted by sudden, sharp noises like that of ringing bells, slamming doors, and barking dogs.

According to Key, these loud silences were a way of manipulating audiences sexually. Key writes, "These silences . . . formed a series of plateaus which gradually increased in volume and decreased in time interval as the story moved towards various dramatic situations . . . [becoming] louder and louder and more rapid as each segment progressed." This sound design, according to Key, left audiences exhausted, nauseated, and/or aroused. He cites a study of fifty women who had seen *The Exorcist*, "over half" of whom admitted that the film "excited them sexually." Key also pointed to "predictable coughing patterns" in audiences, arguing that these coughing fits often occurred directly after these auditory tension peaks as a sort of subconscious tension release, not unlike that of the orgasm. In his view, both the phallic subliminal images and the titillating loud silences cleanly explained the epic mania-producing effects of the film. Their aftershocks, Key writes, "endure far beyond the commercial lifetime of a single movie. What was done to *The Exorcist* audience could endure in some memory systems throughout a lifetime."

Key argues that the passive state of watching a film in a theater—reclined, shrouded in darkness, completely surrendered to the story unfolding before you—makes viewers highly susceptible to dangerous subliminal stimuli. He seems to bear a grudge against the very nature of film itself, an art form that deftly and specifically deploys light and sound in order to provoke a reaction in its viewers. In his condemnation of the film's symbolic imagery and chilling sound design, Key misses something essential and obvious. For me, the functions Key critiques are exactly those a good piece of film should employ. A good film should pull me into its thrall, scramble and distort my brain, and then to spit me back out into the harsh glare of the world, changed in ways it may take me years to fully understand.

According to an interviewee in the documentary *Room 237*, Stanley Kubrick was so inspired by *Subliminal Seduction* that he met with advertising executives in order to pick their brains and better learn how to integrate their subliminal techniques into *The Shining*. He wanted *The Shining* to unsettle viewers in ways that defied easy articulation. If *The Shining* is itself about all of the horrors that both individuals and societies repress—genocide, abuse, colonialism, patriarchy—then what better way to probe and dislodge them than a technology that is itself a kind of repression, a dark and subterranean reality straining to break through to the conscious mind?

•

Warner Bros. did not officially admit to using subliminal images in *The Exorcist* until 1981. Friedkin denied using them until much later. In the era before home video and the pause button, this was an easy thing to deny. In 2012 Friedkin told *Entertainment Weekly*, "You couldn't catch it before VHS. . . . Now you can stop the DVD and stare at it."

Once the subliminal images were acknowledged by the studio, however, a new era of fear around the film emerged. People who had long forgotten *The Exorcist* wondered if they had been living with certain messages subconsciously influencing their minds for years. When I first learned about the subliminal messages in middle school, the idea disturbed me almost as much as my brief exposure to the spider walk had. To think that there were things my brain might have absorbed without my knowing made me feel raw and out of control. I was terrified that somehow, even though I'd only seen that little bit, the horror of *The Exorcist* had been funneled directly into my soul and was slowly but surely turning me into the very monster I dreaded becoming. There was the horror on the surface of the film—the supraliminal horror—and then there was a whole other world of horror throbbing insidiously beneath.

But why this division? Why this fear around the subliminal and this blithe acceptance of the supraliminal? The idea that only the subconscious messages can persuade, distort, and harm is itself a dangerous and manipulative lie. The most threatening messages are often right there on the surface. They don't even bother to hide.

Part 2

✣

SUMMONING THE EVIL SPIRIT

SIX VISIONS OF THE DEVIL
AND HIS DEMONS

In the beginning, Satan was a monstrous assemblage, a sense-less jumble of cloven hooves and membranous wings. Coppo di Marcovaldo's *The Last Judgement* depicts him with giant blue donkey ears from which serpents emerge to snatch naked sinners from their fiery midst. Satan holds a frightened man in each of his outstretched arms. The legs and bare buttocks of another dangle helplessly from Satan's mouth, seconds before the great beast slurps him down.

Here, in one small corner of the mosaic ceiling at the Florence Baptistery, the devil was just beginning to find form. Up until then, Satan had been an absence, a nothing, defined more by what he lacked than by what he was. He emerged from the ineffable as a bestial mess, fragments from the animal world tacked haphazardly onto the human frame.

This Satan's domain is suffering and fear, and he does not work alone. Joining him are the lesser demons. Green men with pronged, serpentine tales. Blue men with pointy beards. Frog-like men crouching as they swallow other men whole. Masters of torture, all of them, skillful and creative in their craft. One roasts a woman on a spit while another slowly dis-embowels her, twirling out her insides like spaghetti on a fork. Other helpless souls are tossed into the roaring flames, which burn their flesh but do not consume it. They will boil there for eternity. Still, the sinners line up, patiently awaiting their fate with quivering hands to their mouths.

Over the centuries, the more monstrous parts of Satan would slowly chip away. In Luca Signorelli's *The Preaching of the Antichrist,* a fresco painted in plague-scourged Orvieto, Satan is the sly and wild-eyed tempter, whispering foul words into the ears of the weak. Satan stands behind a preacher, lips almost touching flesh. This Satan is not without his beastly garnishes—red horns, red wings—but in skin, face, and body, he is undeniably human. He sneaks his arm through the robes of the preacher, curled fingers reaching toward the man's groin. The winking, Mephistophelian seducer, this Satan does not tear your flesh. He shows you all the ways you can tear it yourself.

In the background of Signorelli's vision, the world is in chaos. Angels are cast down from heaven. Dark figures roam about with spears. A person in a sick bed extends her arms to those around her. When Signorelli painted his fresco, the plague was killing millions across Europe. Desperate people declared their devotion to the Lord and then set out on long pilgrimages in search of absolution, spreading the disease along with them.

It was common for the devil and his demons to leave illness in their wake. In Matthias Grünewald's *The Temptation of Saint Anthony,* scaled beasts surround the saint, pecking at him with sharp beaks and grabbing him with yellow, reptilian claws. A naked, crone-like woman with a distended belly and hook nose arches her back in pain. Her blue-tinged skin is covered with infected boils that spurt bright red blood.

Bosch, Schongauer, Ernst, and Dali each tried their hand at depicting Saint Anthony's long temptation in the desert. In all of their creations, Saint Anthony is besieged by foul creatures: elephants with stilt-legs, lizards with bat wings, fish with tiger heads. But what should we make of Grünewald's pestilent crone?

His painting hangs in a small Alsatian convent next to a hospital where patients once went to treat what they then called "Saint Anthony's Fire," or ergot poisoning, now known to be brought on by the ingestion of fungus-contaminated rye grain. In addition to festering boils, this great internal burning caused convulsions and hallucinations, leading some historians to suggest that the young girls and women later accused of witchcraft were really just roiling in ergotism's holy fire.

If the devil wasn't a woman, he was a sinister being whom women worshipped in great numbers. In Francisco Goya's *Witches' Sabbath* or *The Great He-Goat,* a small crowd of grotesque women fall into a trance before a goat-like figure with one oddly human-looking eye. This is one of Goya's *Pinturas negras,* a group of fourteen shadowy and haunting paintings depicting all forms of madness, sickness, and societal disintegration. Goya painted them while living in isolation outside of Madrid, in Carabanchel. He was half-deaf and tormented by his own declining mental and physical health. The figures in these paintings are ugly, shrouded in near absolute darkness. In the rare painting where we see the white glint of a tunic or a bright stroke of blue sky, it is a small blessing.

But Satan wasn't always repulsive or frightening. Sometimes, he was beautiful. In Franz von Stuck's *Lucifer,* Satan is tall and toned, with strong arms and sculpted calves. He sits alone in shadow on a bank of dark stone, perhaps in a cave somewhere in the underworld. He is almost human, save for the large wings that spread out before him like a cloak. These are not the veined wings of a demon, however, but the feathered wings of an angel. Lucifer's eyes are glowing and yellow, with a tiny speck of pupil at their center. Next to him, a shaft of brilliant white light, as if to remind him of his name: light bringer, morning star. Lucifer, the rebel angel who remembers paradise and longs for what he lost. Man would come to relate to this Satan, to see themselves in him. In this Lucifer, we are meant to notice our own bitterness and pride, our own determination and failure, our own thwarted goodness.

Throughout the twentieth century, Satan would shift into many forms: the mustached green trickster selling French aperitifs, a little man brandishing a pitchfork on a tin of ham, a gorgeous woman dressed in red. Satan was no longer the tempter. He was temptation itself. Sometimes, he could even make you laugh.

On the screen in 1973, he briefly invaded the body of a young girl, and once again people were afraid. Satan returned to his long-forgotten status as nonentity, a bodiless nothing in search of a host. In the film, a priest summons Satan from the young girl's body and into his own, but where did Satan go when the priest jumped out of the window and died?

He went into the bodies of dozens of young girls and women just like her, young girls and women who swore and writhed and spewed out the noxious pulp of their insides for all to see. The devil rode into the twenty-first century on their arched and straining backs, vaulted skyward as if they could kiss the heavens with their ice-cold skin.

MAGICAL MIRRORS

No one wanted Ellen Burstyn to play Chris MacNeil, the mother of the possessed child in *The Exorcist*. Though Burstyn actively campaigned for the role, Ted Ashley, the Warner Bros. chairperson, rather vociferously declared that he'd give Burstyn the role "over my dead body." The studio wanted Jane Fonda, who had just won an Oscar playing a prostitute-turned-spy in *Klute*. "Why would I want to be in a piece of capitalist rip-off bullshit?" Fonda is rumored to have said when offered the part, shortly before jetting off to Vietnam and earning the nickname "Hanoi Jane." Anne Bancroft passed on the role shortly after that, as did Audrey Hepburn, who was in Rome with her Italian husband at the time and didn't want to piss off the Pope. When all the other actresses fell through, Burstyn at last got the part. Perhaps she saw an opportunity in the still disreputable horror genre that these other actresses did not. After all, *The Exorcist* is one of the few New Hollywood films in which a single woman and her adolescent daughter play prominent roles and receive just as much, if not more, screen time than the two leading men.

It is likely no surprise that the seventies were a thrilling time for film but not a particularly thrilling time for the women in those films. Despite the progress of second-wave feminism, the New Hollywood of the late 1960s and '70s was a largely reactionary movement dominated by men in every way imaginable. In *From Reverence to Rape,* critic and film historian Molly Haskell calls the decade a "painful transition period" during which men, "deprived of the physical grounds for testing their virility and those magical mirrors women held up to their egos," used film to redefine their masculinity and put women back in their place. Though there are of course important exceptions to the rule, especially when women also served as directors, producers, or screenwriters—*Wanda, A Women Under the Influence, Alice Doesn't Live Here Anymore, Girlfriends,* and *Five Easy Pieces,* for example—actresses in the 1970s were steadily ousted from their shining spots at the center of the star system and pushed to the sidelines with roles as dowdy mothers, nagging wives, or hollow sex objects, all while male violence and machismo was amplified, glorified, and transformed into high art. Gangster films like *Mean Streets* and *The Godfather* reinvigorated ideals of masculine authority and strength while road films like *Easy Rider, Five Easy Pieces,* and *Two-Lane Blacktop* showed alienated male heroes breaking away from the suffocating confines of middle-class family life, rejecting work and marriage to find freedom and pleasure on the American highway. As Haskell writes, "In the road films, the women are lucky to be mere bodies, way stations where the heroes can relieve themselves and resume their journey." Haskell argues that film in this decade became a testing ground for men to create and explore new definitions of masculinity in the face of a growing feminist uproar. Even with the long-overdue changes taking place in their personal and political lives, women in film were forced back into the very roles they were rallying against. Ellen Burstyn has admitted that after filming *The Exorcist,* she struggled to find a role where the woman "wasn't either the victim, running away from a predator, or a prostitute."

The Exorcist premiered at a potent moment for the women's liberation movement. The Equal Rights Amendment, which would guarantee equal rights for all Americans regardless of sex, was just setting out on its lengthy and ongoing path toward ratification. *Fear of Flying* by Erica Jong shocked and angered the public with its boldly honest depiction of female sexuality, fantasy, and rage. *Ms.* magazine was in its second year of circulation, appearing alongside *Good Housekeeping* on magazine racks in grocery stores with cover stories like "The Housewife's Moment of Truth" and "Wonder Woman for President." Title IX had recently made it illegal for public schools to bar girls from participating in sports or any other activity. Not long after, Billie Jean King defeated Bobby Riggs in the infamous "Battle of the Sexes" tennis tournament, destabilizing the long-held belief in women's physical inferiority. Though women still couldn't open a credit card in their own name or take legal action against workplace harassment or spousal rape, they could now serve in the military and on a jury in all fifty states. By 1973 they could also apply for an Ivy League education at Yale, Princeton, Dartmouth, and Brown (Columbia, on the other hand, would hold out until 1988). Perhaps most fittingly, *The Exorcist,* a gruesome horror story about an adolescent female body invaded by an outside force that must be brutally isolated and expelled, premiered almost one year to the day after *Roe v. Wade* established a woman's legal right to abortion.

In *Danse Macabre,* Stephen King says of his classic 1974 menstrual panic bloodbath, *Carrie,* "Writing the book in 1973 and out of college three years, I was fully aware of what Women's Liberation implied for me and others of my sex. The book is, in its more adult implications, an uneasy masculine shrinking away from female equality." *The Exorcist,* another horror film that casts the maturing female body as a mutinous hotbed of evil and excess, takes this masculine unease one step further. Whereas Carrie is perhaps the most powerful individual in her film, gaining supernatural strength and ecstatically destroying those who have wronged her, *The Exorcist* reduces its adolescent female to a hysterical body trapped in a bed, her inner life of pain, fear, joy, and desire completely unknown to the audience. For all its problems, *Carrie* at least encourages viewers to feel some amount of sympathy for its monster, who is humiliated and bullied at school and manipulated and abused by her mother at home. No such sympathy system exists for Regan. As a thinking and feeling human being, she is nonexistent. She is only a body to fear.

Though she gets the most critical attention, Regan was not the only part of *The Exorcist* that shocked audiences in 1973. Her mother, Chris MacNeil, a divorced actress with short-cropped hair and a biting temper, also represented a threat to traditional American values of female domesticity, passivity, and idealized motherhood. A single, working woman making "80 thou" a year, as the novel describes it, Chris is rich enough to rent a beautiful house on Prospect Street while in Georgetown shooting the film *Crash Course,* which centers on campus free speech protests. She hires a butler, a maid, and a personal assistant to help with the more mundane duties she can't be bothered to do herself. In fact, Regan spends much of her time with Chris's pantsuit-wearing assistant, Sharon (played by Kitty Winn, whose short-lived film career spanned 1971–78). Chris's life with Regan is illustrious and unconventional, filled with red-carpet events, trips to Europe, and even invitations to the White House. Chris is very much a member of the bourgeoisie, a second-wave feminist at its whitest and most privileged. Perhaps most disturbing of all, she does not believe in God. Chris turns to the Catholic Church for help with her unwell daughter only after all other solutions—a pediatrician, psychiatrist, and hypnotist—have proved useless.

As played by Burstyn, Chris MacNeil is gruff and commanding. She swears often, seldom smiles, and does not seem at all inclined to please or pacify anyone (except perhaps her daughter, whom she unquestionably adores). Chris has no romantic partners in the film and seems to have little interest in obtaining one, though there is noticeable tension between her and Father Karras, the priest. Ted Ashley, as it turns out, was completely wrong in not wanting Burstyn to play the part. She is perfect, fittingly lacking Jane Fonda's righteous flirtatiousness, Anne Bancroft's simmering sexuality, or Aubrey Hepburn's childlike elegance. Very little about Burstyn fulfills audience expectations of what a woman should be, creating an unconscious uneasiness in audiences accustomed to consuming films of the era in which most actresses were little more than beautiful and high-functioning props. Long before the concept of "women's rage" was seen as palatable or profitable, Chris's easy anger and lack of warmth must have struck many viewers as an unseemly threat.

In fact, *The Exorcist* can be seen as a graphic warning call to women like Chris who dare to drift outside the realm of male control. By horror movie logic, the female-led household in *The Exorcist*, much like the one in *Carrie*, is inherently more penetrable, more open to invasion by an evil outside force, than a household with a strong male at the helm. Without the presence of a masculine authority figure to guide and protect, the theory goes, the aberrant home will descend into chaos and moral disorder. It is only through the intervention of two male priests that the evil is purged and order is at last restored. In the end, *The Exorcist* is a story of female weakness and male valor. Both Father Karras and Father Merrin die after exorcising the demon from Regan's body and are therefore transformed into valiant heroes who sacrifice themselves in order to save the film's wayward, malevolent females from a torment of their own making. Chris is helpless before her daughter's plight because she is in fact its cause. In this way, Regan becomes the heinous end result of women's liberation, a helpless, growling embodiment of what feminism, the sexual revolution, and civil rights will do to the nation's nicest, happiest, and whitest youth.

•

Mrs. Rosemary Mayers taught computer literacy at my Oregon grade school, Sacred Trinity, in the 1990s. To this day, I credit her with my impressive typing speeds and profound love of making PowerPoint presentations. Mrs. Mayers demystified computers and their various programs with approachable ease, turning a blank Excel spreadsheet into something boundlessly exciting and full of opportunity. When we weren't learning how to navigate search engines and master Microsoft Word, we were navigating the pixelated plains of the American West on *The Oregon Trail,* where we named passengers after our enemies and took great pride when they died quickly and brutally of dysentery. As young Oregonians ourselves, we felt the game was made especially for us—I learned only years later that children from other states played the game too. *The Oregon Trail* was a way of normalizing and romanticizing our status as settlers, of indebting us to the bonnet-wearing forbearers who suffered spectacular hardship so that we could one day attend the very suburban Catholic grade school where we reenacted their suffering on an endless, neon green loop.

For all its drama and river fording, however, *The Oregon Trail* was a lark in comparison to the much more pressing danger Mrs. Mayers told us was lurking elsewhere, in the dark and expanding netherworld of the internet. The door to the computer lab was almost always open, allowing air from the hallways to flow into the tiny, whirring classroom, but sometimes, when the urge struck, Mrs. Mayers would slam the door shut with a loud bang, revealing the black-and-white poster she had taped to the back of it.

"*This*," Mrs. Mayers would say, "is who is waiting when you talk to strangers online."

The poster depicted a shirtless man staring at us from behind overgrown white eyebrows. His leathery arms were tattooed with hearts and anchors. With one hand, he fingered the skinny rattail that slithered over his bare and bony shoulder. With the other, he smoked a cigarette out of a gaping stoma. Behind him, a computer screen glowed ominously, as if a child was trapped inside it, begging to be set free.

Every one of Mrs. Mayers's lectures began this way, with the jarring slam and the door warning. The man on the poster, with his deflated nipples and lustful gaze, epitomized the soulless pedophile I was taught to believe lurked in chat rooms and white vans, waiting to strike. These lectures were fervent and sincere; Mrs. Mayers really did believe in her mission of saving us from the internet's nicotine-stained perverts and murderers. She was merely doing her duty as a teacher, a parent, and most importantly, an adult. However, her lectures about how the internet was the most dangerous place on earth to be a child were somewhat confusing, as my grade-school self was already under the impression that the earth was the most dangerous place to be a child, period.

There was always some kidnapped white girl on Oprah or the evening news who I feared would one day be me. I lived convinced that I was just one slashed window screen away from being secreted deep into the woods and chained inside a tent for months on end, beaten, raped, and starved. Mixed in with this fear was a certain romantic fascination with these kidnapped children, a secret hope that I might one day become one of them. When I was ten, two young girls, Miranda Gaddis and Ashley Pond, were kidnapped and murdered by Ward Weaver III, their bodies kept in a fifty-five-gallon drum hidden beneath a concrete slab in his backyard. After constantly seeing the story on the local news for a few weeks, I went out and bought a choker necklace just like the one Ashley wore in her school picture. Being kidnapped seemed like the most effective way to get a large number of people to care about me. I wanted my smiling school picture to appear on the TV every night, for people across the country to know my name. I wanted my sobbing parents to stand before a phalanx of microphones and beg the nation to help them find their little girl.

Perhaps more so, I was compelled by the sense of an adventure that kidnapping seemed to offer. I would often fantasize about being kept for weeks in a small, dark space, plotting my harrowing escape. I knew that if the cops ever approached me in the public library while my captor stood by my side, I would scream my name and shout, "Help!" I wouldn't shake my head and let the officers walk away like that weakling Elizabeth Smart did. I distinctly remember watching an E! news special about a girl who escaped from her abductor by sneaking beneath the room service trolley when he took her to a hotel for the night. I envisioned some tense, inventive escape like that, and then the triumph of my return: my glowing mother bending down to sweep me into her arms, her hot tears wetting my unwashed hair as her happy laughter pounded through my body, and me, gleeful and heroic, scarred but finally free.

In this frenzied atmosphere of high-profile kidnappings and online predators, I developed an odd relationship to my own childhood. Though I was a middle-class white kid living in the monolithic fortress of the Portland suburbs with a stay-at-home mom who picked me up from my private Catholic school every day promptly at 3:00 p.m., I believed I was constantly in danger of the most unspeakable horrors. I feared being cruelly wrestled from the safety of my family at the same time that I lusted after the attention such a tragedy would bring. Elizabeth Smart got to meet Oprah, after all. People applauded and cried when she took to the stage. She was special, forever marked by the enticing twin traumas of pain and fame.

My brother Charley and I would watch these afternoon talk shows and evening specials with my mother every day after school. She'd always hold us a little closer on the couch and kiss our forehead during them, as if to remind herself she needed to do everything in her power—move to the suburbs, quit nursing, send us to Catholic School—to keep her children safe. I would curl up inside myself before the screen, afraid of the world and yet ready to fulfill the destiny I was told waited for me in the city streets, or the school playground, or in the cold dark of night.

●

"Remember the movie *The Exorcist*? The film?" asks Geraldo Rivera in his 1988 multipart TV special *Devil Worship: Exposing Satan's Underground*. "It dealt with ridding the body of Satan in a ritual called exorcism."

Throughout the special, Rivera stands before a wall of TVs, individual faces grimly flickering from each. On one screen, we see Sean Sellers, described by Rivera as "an all-American boy," who is waiting to be interviewed from his cell on Oklahoma's death row. On another screen, we see Charles Gervais, a man serving a life sentence in Louisiana State Penitentiary for allegedly sewing his victim's body into a couch and dumping it into a swamp. On yet another screen waits Ozzy Osbourne, the so-called Prince of Darkness, who sang songs about witches and black masses, songs with lyrics like, "Look into my eyes, you will see who I am / I am Lucifer, please take my hand." On the stage, alongside the host, sits a Catholic priest, Anton Lavey's daughter Zeena, and Michael Aquino, the founder of the Temple of Set. In the audience: journalists, representatives from the victim's rights organization Believe the Children, and veteran FBI agent and cult investigator Ted Gunderson.

The Exorcist is mentioned only once in the course of the entire series, but it looms large over every episode. The special begins, not unlike Johnny Carson's warning about *The Exorcist* some fifteen years before, with the sobering disclaimer: "The very young and impressionable definitely should not be watching this program tonight." Throughout the series, Geraldo recounts a string of increasingly outlandish tales: fathers wearing baby feet around their necks, high school boys beating their classmate with a bat "just because he was a human," and young killers drinking the blood of their victim in a barn while heavy metal blares. The series lavishes special attention on the white men who supposedly murdered innocent victims in the name of Satan, including Sellers and Gervais but also Charles Manson and David Berkowitz, the so-called Son of Sam, who once claimed to have been heavily influenced by *The Exorcist* himself.

"No place in America is beyond the reach of devil worshippers," Geraldo repeatedly warns his millions of viewers.

Devil worshipers lurked in even the most unexpected of American places: small town churches, quiet suburban neighborhoods, the upper echelons of the military. However, the most dangerous places in America, if you listened to people like Geraldo, were the steadily growing number of private day cares cropping up across the nation.

In 1971 Nixon vetoed the Comprehensive Child Development Act, which would have established a national day care system to aid working parents and alleviate the mounting pressure on the country's embattled welfare system. If the bill had passed, parents would have been charged for childcare on a sliding scale based on their ability to pay. Along with basic childcare, the centers would have provided a suite of dental, medical, nutritional, and counseling services. In his rationale for vetoing the bill, Nixon employed timeworn red-baiting rhetoric to argue that a national day care system would erode the nuclear family and establish a dangerous "communal approach to child rearing," the very thing many feminists and gay and lesbian activists saw as the key to their freedom.

Nearly identical logic has been used to discredit universal day care in recent years. In April 2021, during renewed talks about the state of childcare in the United States, Tennessee senator Marsha Blackburn tweeted a link to a 1974 *New York Times* article about free day care services in the Soviet Union. Idaho state representative Charlie Shepherd has said of universal day care, "Anything that makes it easier or more convenient for women to get out of the home, I don't think that's a good direction for us to be going."

As a result of the failure of the Comprehensive Child Development Act, private day care centers began opening up all across the country, welcoming the children of the many single or working mothers who entered the workforce throughout the decade. By 1983, twelve years after the bill's failure and ten years after the premiere of *The Exorcist,* these day cares served as one of the Satanic panic's most useful and enduring points of hysteria.

Starting with the 1983 McMartin preschool scandal in Manhattan Beach, news stories sprouted everywhere about devil-worshiping day care workers physically and sexually abusing the young children they were paid to keep safe. Most of these accusations developed out of small truths, such as a day care worker spanking a child. Concerned parents, the burgeoning victim's rights movement, and the newly minted twenty-four-hour news cycle then whipped these stories into a noxious frenzy. Oprah took a cue from Geraldo too, interviewing the crown princess of the Satanic panic, Michelle Smith, in 1989, nearly ten years after her memoir, *Michelle Remembers*, was published. In the book, Michelle graphically recounts her torturous upbringing in a satanic cult using the repressed memories she was able to retrieve with help from her therapist-turned-husband-turned-coauthor, Dr. Lawrence Pazder. If Geraldo's special sent a clear message that the nation's youth were constantly in danger of the most sickening forms of sexual and physical abuse, *Michelle Remembers* convinced some adults that they might have once been victims too, even if the knowledge of it was still waiting latent in their subconscious.

It didn't matter that most acts of child abuse, including sexual abuse, are committed by relatives or friends, or that Satanism as an ideology has far less to do with violence and demonic worship than it does personal liberation and opposition to Christian doctrine, or that scant physical evidence was ever found to corroborate any of the Satanic panic's most outlandish claims. Moral panics do not operate out of fact but out of ignorance and fear, mobilizing blatantly obvious fictions to keep the existing order safe. As Paul M. Renfro writes in *Stranger Danger: Family Values, Childhood, and the American Carceral State,* the hysteria around child abduction and abuse was a reaction to the "perceived moral rot unleashed by 60s and 70s liberationism" in which "economic and political instability, alongside the reconfiguration of cultural and sexual norms, had supposedly disrupted the idealized white American family and the child upon which it hinged." By the time I was born in the early '90s, the innocent American child—almost always white, photogenic, and middle-class—was perceived as a pressing cause around which the entire nation should rally to protect.

This effort, of course, was selective. The child abduction and abuse panic unfolded during, and in fact fueled, an unprecedented expansion of the nation's carceral and surveillance state, which quickly ensnared Black youth in its ever-evolving punitive net. While white children were elevated as pure innocents constantly at risk of unimaginable abuse, Black children were largely deemed "super-predators" and increasingly tossed into prison, often for life.

•

A fiercely conservative and anti-Semitic impulse, Satan as a cultural boogeyman tends to emerge whenever society is perceived to be swinging leftward, providing traditional factions with an excuse to cast any signs of "progress" as harbingers of evil. If the original Satanic panic erupted partly in response to women making professional strides outside of the home, a similar panic began to smolder just as the first woman in American history came dangerously close to shattering the executive ceiling. This time around, however, rather than infecting the small institutions of middle-class American life, Satanists had at last gained control of the most exclusive channels of American power, allowing our nation's leaders to corrupt good and decent Americans on a scale day care workers and *Dungeons & Dragons* aficionados could only have dreamed of a few decades before.

The epicenter of the latest round of satanic paranoia was, of course, Hillary Clinton. According to the conspiracy theories that began popping up around the time of the 2016 election, Hillary Clinton was a murderous, paraphilic Satanist with a body count that put Ted Bundy to shame. During the campaign, stories quickly began to spread that Clinton was part of a vast network of corrupt devil worshipers stretching from Hollywood to DC, who liked to sip on cocktails of semen and baby's blood while planning the enslavement of the God-fearing American people. Unsubstantiated stories about crucified babies and sex-trafficked children once again seized the attention of a distressing number of American citizens, forming a dangerously seductive far-right counterweight to growing movements like Black Lives Matter and #MeToo.

Conspiracy theories and moral panics like QAnon tend to ignore the very real dangers facing the groups they claim to care about in favor of outlandish tales centered on conveniently invented enemies. For example, most instances of sex trafficking happen to young people abandoned by their families, often due to their sexual orientation or gender identity, not to suburban children supported and protected by their loved ones. Focusing on stories about satanic murder or child sex trafficking allows us to deflect, to focus all our rage on a rare and often imagined crime rather than on real, structural causes of youth suffering or on the hallowed institutions—such as the Boy Scouts of America or the Catholic Church—that have escaped true accountability for years.

•

Abuse interpretations of *The Exorcist* are not uncommon online, where armchair film theorists cast Regan not as a monster but as a helpless young victim locked in a dark room, alone. One video available on YouTube called "The Even Darker Underbelly of *The Exorcist*" explores the "possible sexual abuse themes in one of the most famous and highly sexualized horror films of all time." The video argues that Regan manifests "all the major symptoms of childhood sexual abuse," including "inappropriate sexual conduct, sexually offensive vocabulary, insomnia, lying, tantrums, involuntary urinating, depression, self-probing with a foreign object, distrust of opposite sex adults, and violence and hostility." The video suggests that *The Exorcist* can be read as a surrealist interpretation of sexual abuse symptoms, or that viewers are simply imposing their supernatural readings onto what is clearly a tale of post-abuse trauma. Much of its analysis focuses on the often-inebriated movie director, Burke Dennings, who, in addition to directing the film *Crash Course*, is good friends with Chris and therefore often hangs out around both her and Regan. Burke eventually falls to his death from the window in Regan's room. The movie suggests but never explicitly says that the possessed Regan killed him. But the question remains: Why was Burke in a twelve-year-old girl's room in the first place?

I find this interpretation interesting and not, at first blush, outlandish or problematic. However, take it a few steps further and you can easily fit a QAnon-style reading onto the film. Could Burke possibly be a member of the corrupt Hollywood elite, using the helpless Regan to fulfill his perverse impulses? Does Regan kill him in order to save herself from being transported via underground tunnels to the various politicians and powerbrokers of Washington, DC, who also want to have their pedophilic way with her? And is her single, atheist mother, Chris MacNeil, a famous actress with an open invitation to the White House, somehow implicated in it all? With her short-cropped hair, perfectly tailored pantsuits, and proud lack of warm domesticity, doesn't Chris MacNeil resemble, in her own way, Hillary Clinton?

The jump is easier to make then you might think.

One summer day in 2016, I was walking in downtown Portland when I saw a poster for a documentary called *Hillary's America*, directed by far-right firebrand Dinesh D'Souza. *Hillary's America* was one of the most popular documentaries of 2016, grossing a whopping $5.6 million dollars in the first dozen days of its release. The movie, a corny, reenactment-filled follow-up to *Obama's America,* D'Souza's previous, anti-Obama film, basically argues that the Democratic Party, once the party of slaveholders, is now bent on enslaving us all to the federal government. It dares to ask the hard-hitting question: "What if the goal of the Democratic Party is to steal the most valuable thing the world has ever produced? What if their plan is to steal America?"

The chief architect of this heist is, of course, Hillary Clinton. In the poster for *Hillary's America,* Clinton stands in front of a fawning crowd, looking very much the demagogue. Her arms are spread in a gesture of both triumph and self-love: she has fooled and brainwashed the American people, and she's loving it. The entire poster has a gaudy, purple-pink tint to it that is feminine and menacing at the same time. In the background lurks an even larger reproduction of Hillary's face, her eyes glaring and glowing, the bags under them as hideous and exaggerated as the drooping wrinkles around her mouth.

I stood in front of the poster for a solid minute or so, both amused and annoyed. Its agenda was so shameless you almost had to laugh. I would have too, if it hadn't been for the quote located at the top of the poster, directly above Hillary's ominous, glowing purple eyes.

"Utterly terrifying—and based on a true story," it said.

Beneath the quote, its attribution: William Peter Blatty, author and screenwriter of *The Exorcist.*

I felt shocked when I saw it. I didn't want to believe it. There's part of me that still doesn't. It's hard to credibly believe anything about the film *Hillary's America,* even the attribution on its poster. Still, I know that Blatty was a deeply conservative Catholic who seemed to become even more conservative later in life. In 2012 he filed a canon law petition against his

alma mater, Georgetown, for, among other things, inviting pro-
ponents of abortion rights to speak at the university, which
he saw as a stark perversion of Catholic doctrine. It's not
unthinkable that Blatty would be drawn to a ludicrous piece of
right-wing propaganda in his old age.

I nonetheless feel an abiding fondness for Blatty. I'm
warmed by the self-effacing humor in his memoirs, and I can
relate to his life-consuming need to tell the story that obsessed
him. In fact, I believe him when he says he wrote *The Exorcist* to comfort audiences, to show them the endless power
and grace of God. But stories have a life outside their author's
intentions. Like any piece of art, *The Exorcist* was influenced
by cultural forces and subconscious anxieties that Blatty could
not have necessarily perceived in himself but that nonetheless were present each time he put pen to paper. Seeing that
poster of *Hillary's America* in 2016 reminded me that a fear
of women and a backlash to their political, cultural, and economic advancement animates every page and frame of *The
Exorcist* with a force that endures to this day.

•

The year after *The Exorcist* premiered, Ellen Burstyn won an
Academy Award for her performance in the 1974 film *Alice
Doesn't Live Here Anymore*. Executives at Warner Bros. had
come around to Burstyn after watching dailies from *The Exorcist* during production, and they told her they wanted to make
another project with her after *The Exorcist* wrapped. Though
Burstyn quickly began searching for a script, she found that
almost everything her agent presented to her involved female
characters who were either supportive housewives, selfless
mothers, or helpless victims of some form of horrendous sexual or physical abuse. She told Bob Costas in 1992 that these
female characters were "somebody's idea of what a woman is,

but not anything that I recognized." When her agent finally discovered Robert Getchell's script for *Alice Doesn't Live Here Anymore,* a quiet drama about a widow who starts a new life in the American Southwest, Burstyn quickly signed on as both lead actress and executive producer. Francis Ford Coppola introduced Burstyn to Martin Scorsese, and Scorsese signed on to direct what would become one of the few films in his decades-long career with a female at its center.

In the film, a housewife named Alice moves to Arizona with her young son after her volatile and borderline abusive husband is killed in a car accident. Though the newly single Alice initially plans to relocate to her childhood home of Monterey to pursue her long-abandoned dreams of becoming a singer, her money quickly dries up, and she is forced to take a waitressing job at a diner in Tucson. There, she meets and eventually falls in love with David, a cheery rancher played by Kris Kristofferson.

Alice Doesn't Live Here Anymore is an understated, intimate film about a woman unmoored from the life she thought she would and should have: one of domesticity, motherhood, and quiet, unarticulated dissatisfaction. The film and other similar "domestic refusenik" dramas of the era, such as *Wanda* and *Diary of a Mad Housewife,* are a necessary feminine counterweight to the male-centered road films of the era, in which men broke from the deadening confines of domestic family life to find freedom and exhilaration on the open highway. In *Alice Doesn't Live Here Anymore,* this independence is thrust upon Alice, and she finds that her newfound liberation is often confusing, difficult, and ripe with internal conflict. For Alice, there is no clean and triumphant trajectory from "housewife" to "strong, liberated woman." No longer wholly defined by her roles as wife and mother, Alice must begin the bumpy and complicated project of defining herself.

For obvious reasons, *Alice Doesn't Here Anymore* is one of Scorsese's lesser-known works. Though the film features some classic Scorsese touches (rock music, roving cameras, and Harvey Keitel), it lacks the operatic violence and masculine grit that draws so many people to his films. Thanks in part to Ellen Burstyn's creative influence, as well as Marcia Lucas's editing and Toby Rafelson's production design, *Alice Doesn't Live Here Anymore* is a nuanced, funny, and deeply feminine film that explores the "painful transition period," to borrow Molly Haskell's words, when women began reevaluating themselves and the roles they'd been told they should fill.

If *The Exorcist* is a reactionary film that vividly and gruesomely reflects male fears of women's liberation and its accompanying threat to the nuclear family and other traditional values, *Alice Doesn't Live Here Anymore* reflects the pleasures, perils, and struggles of women's liberation from a wholly female perspective. Alice's son is not traumatized or endangered by her newfound independence. Even when he gets drunk off Ripple with his rebellious friend Audrey (played by Jodie Foster) and winds up in a police holding cell, he remains a smart and playful kid who clearly loves his mother and is happy to watch her build a life of her own. Perhaps after making *The Exorcist*, a film she had to fight hard just to be cast in, Burstyn no longer wanted to make films that held mirrors up to men's notorious egos, paranoias, and insecurities.

There is no warning call in *Alice Doesn't Live Here Anymore*. Rather, there's a gentle reminder that though liberation is difficult, and though there are forces both internal and external constantly conspiring to keep women in their place, the work is radical and necessary and still unfinished.

SOMETHING SHARP

Chris and Regan are alone in the basement of their rental house on 3600 Prospect Street. Regan, dressed in blue jeans and a knit sweater, is showing off her newest art project: a bright yellow papier-mâché bird. Regan is crafty, and though 3600 Prospect Street is not their permanent home, she has already littered her various creations throughout the house. Drawings cover the walls. Tiny clay sculptures of turtles and squirrels crowd the windowsills.

Some viewers have suggested that the bird, with its phallic beak and expansive wings, is a visual echo to the demon Pazuzu we see in the desert at the beginning of the film. Regan is not yet showing any obvious signs of demonic possession, but she is looking older, more mature, in ways that sometimes shock and sadden her mother. In the next scene, Chris will find an old tabloid in Regan's bedroom—the two of them are on the cover—and she'll scoff.

"You look so old here," she'll say. It almost makes her angry, the way her daughter is growing up without her permission. Chris knows she has to cling to these rare and easy moments of intimacy and warmth before they disappear forever.

In the basement, Chris pulls out a dusty old ouija board.

Regan tells her mother that she found it when they first moved into the rental house and has been using it to communicate with a supernatural being named Captain Howdy.

"I think you need two people to play," Chris tells Regan, as if to gently suggest that there is no Captain Howdy, that it is all in her overly imaginative daughter's head.

"No, I don't," Regan responds knowingly, holding the planchette to the board. "I do it all the time."

•

The story goes something like this.

William Friedkin needed to find the right little girl for his film. She had to be strong and stable, good humored and intelligent, someone who could say lines like "Let Jesus fuck you" and not be left irreparably damaged. Friedkin didn't want any responsibility for setting some innocent little girl off on the wrong path for life. The filmmaker was entering uncharted cinematic territory, and he must have paused, or at least we hope, to consider an important question: What will playing the devil incarnate do to a young child? As he started his search, Friedkin knew at least this much: the little girl had to be a good actress, and of course, she had to be pretty.

In the book version of *The Exorcist,* Regan has freckles, red hair, and braces, just like I did when I turned twelve. Friedkin would take certain artistic liberties when casting his Regan, preferring tall, snub-nosed brunettes. He spent months searching, flipping through stack after stack of sunny young actresses, all white, shiny, and smiling. He'd bring the ones he liked into his office for an audition, but none of them were quite right. Some seemed too immature to handle the intensity of the role; others were promising, but their parents balked at the image of their sweet daughter transforming into a monster. Even the most fame-hungry stage parent thought such a role would hurt, not elevate, their child's burgeoning career. Mike Nichols had passed on the project because he didn't want the success of the film to depend on the performance of an untrained child. Friedkin was starting to think Nichols was right. But then round-faced Linda Blair walked into his office.

Friedkin was a big name around Hollywood in those days, and working with an Academy Award–winning director could open serious doors for an aspiring actress, even one who up to that point had only landed a few child modeling gigs and a small role in the short-lived soap opera *Hidden Faces*. Linda Blair, born just a few months before my mother in 1959, was a sweet-natured, horse-loving child actress living in Connecticut with dreams of staring in movies about princesses, about little girls and their dogs. If she hadn't made it as an actress, Blair would have been perfectly content growing up to be a jockey or a veterinarian. Getting cast by someone as illustrious as William Friedkin, with his tinted aviator glasses and gargantuan ego, was certainly a long shot, but Linda's mother took her daughter to the audition anyway. The Blair's old address in St. Louis must have seemed like an omen: 123 Hollywood Lane. Friedkin had auditioned countless girls and liked none of them, so maybe, just maybe, Linda had a chance.

When Linda and her mother arrived at Friedkin's Manhattan office, William asked a few basic questions and then went over the script, discussing in detail some of the things Linda would be required to do if she were cast. When they approached the scene where Regan masturbates with the crucifix, William paused and prepared to ask what he had asked stacks of other girls before her. He took a deep breath.

"Linda," he said. "Do you understand what Regan is doing here?"

"Yeah," Linda responded eagerly, as if she were in class

and knew she had the answer the teacher wanted. "She's masturbating."

William nodded.

"And do you know what masturbating is, Linda?"

"It's like jerking off," Linda replied.

"And have you ever masturbated before?" William asked, shooting Linda's mother a tentative, apologetic glance.

"Sure, of course I have," Linda said. "Hasn't everyone?"

With that, Friedkin smiled and leaned back in his chair. His search, at last, could end.

Pauline Kael mentioned this story in her 1974 review of *The Exorcist*. She describes Linda Blair as a "sparkling, snub-nosed, happy-looking little girl, who matches up perfectly with Ellen Burstyn." Kael adds, "I wonder about those four hundred and ninety-nine mothers of the rejected little girls. . . . They must have read the novel; they must have known what they were having their beautiful little daughters tested for. When they see *The Exorcist* and watch Linda Blair urinating on the fancy carpet and screaming and jabbing at herself with the crucifix, are they envious? Do they feel, 'That might have been my little Susie—famous forever?'"

●

In the notorious scene, vinyl records swirl through the room in a manic cyclone. Curtains slap wildly against the window-pane. The girl's mother rushes in and finds her daughter sitting upright in bed on her knees, stabbing herself repeatedly with a crucifix until she spurts bright red blood. It makes a horrible sound, like a dull knife goring through ripe fruit. You can just imagine the foley artists in postproduction going at a grape-fruit like mad. The motion, and the slight thrust of the little girl's hips as she does it, is violent, greedy, wrong. As she stabs herself, the little girl growls "Let Jesus fuck you" again and again, her eyes frantic and wide.

Chris rushes over to Regan and tries to grab the crucifix from her hand. Instead, the girl yanks her mother's head into her bloody crotch and holds it there. "Eat me! Eat me!" she barks. When Chris surfaces, her frightened face is stained with her daughter's blood. Regan then punches her mother with a strength well beyond that of a twelve-year-old girl. Chris's body hits the back wall with a loud thud. A dresser barrels inexplicably toward where she cowers in the corner, presumably propelled by the demonic force thrashing inside Regan. Chris gasps and dashes away just in time. For all the cultural fervor around the crucifix-masturbation scene, few people ever bother to point out that Regan also comes frighteningly close to committing matricide.

Before she leaves the room, Chris takes one last look and sees her daughter's head spin slowly around, a full 360 degrees. The camera zooms up on the girl's face—teeth jagged, skin pale, eyes not quite human—as she growls, "Do you know what she did? Your cunting daughter?"

William Peter Blatty considered this scene a necessary solution to a nagging plot problem: What is so horrible that it would drive an atheist to a priest? He had already done so much work establishing Chris as a logical and devoted nonbeliever that any sudden and dramatic conversion would seem entirely out of character. To make the plot progress in a logical way, Blatty needed a moment so appalling and unexpected that Chris would finally accept that something supernatural was at work. It had to shock her conscience into belief. And what is worse to imagine, in a country simultaneously puritanical and perverse, than a violently masturbating little girl?

The scene would not only solve a thorny narrative issue, it would also prove commercially viable: The crucifix-masturbation scene was an undeniable audience draw. Many people paid to see *The Exorcist* solely because, thanks to the dissolution of the Motion Picture Production Code five years before, they could now watch something so graphic and shocking play out on an American screen.

A little girl, they must have whispered, *masturbating with a crucifix.*

•

As a child, I was a brazen and enthusiastic masturbator. I discovered masturbation early, well before the first grade, and I would do it anywhere and everywhere I pleased: while watching *Aladdin* on the family room couch, seated in the backseat of the car on the drive home from the grocery store, in the bathroom before dinner when I was supposed to be washing my hands. Mostly though, I did it at night. As a troubled sleeper, both before and after I saw those fatal frames from *The Exorcist,* something about the dizzying rise and warm rush of the act always lulled me to sleep.

For much of my early childhood, I masturbated brashly, regularly, and efficiently. It felt as normal and necessary as scratching an itch. The desire was mostly unattached to any object, a free-floating thing to be caught and quenched as needed. Rarely, if ever, was the desire associated with a living person I knew. In kindergarten, when I developed my first crush on Drew McGaw, a curly-haired boy who drank goat's milk and wore argyle sweaters, he never once excited any of my autoerotic urges. I mostly wanted nothing to do with boys, whose back teeth seemed permanently caked with black Oreo crumbs.

Occasionally, however, I noticed the urge arising in response to certain things I saw on the screen: Leonardo DiCaprio in *Growing Pains,* adolescent Link in the *Legend of Zelda: Oca-*

rina of Time, the toaster in *Brave Little Toaster,* especially the moment when it unplugs itself from the socket and scurries off, chord trailing behind. Even certain Beanie Babies, the Princess Diana one in particular, could set me off. Its velvety purple coat stirred something deep inside of me, and I still suspect this is why some adults are now willing to drop twenty grand on eBay for a mint-condition 1997 original.

I was caught in the act only once, though I suspect my parents knew more than they let on. It was late at night, and I was lying in bed with my grandma Nanie, who I thought had fallen asleep. Just as I was reaching that feverish peak, Nanie ripped up the covers, looked down, and said, with both shock and fear twisting her voice, "Stop touching yourself!" When I picture the scene now, I imagine her saying it with the same crazed agony of Brad Pitt in *Seven* asking Kevin Spacey what's in the box. I froze, like a panicked prey animal. There was a brief moment of tension in the dark before Nanie rolled over and presumably fell back asleep.

It was a lesson I would have had to learn sooner or later: One generally should not masturbate in front of one's grandparent. In retrospect, things could have gone much worse. I wasn't punished, and the incident was never discussed again. Still, it lingers in my memory as the moment when my glorious onanistic bubble burst and in its place doubt and shame flooded in.

●

The idea that a child, especially a female child, can engage in any type of sexual activity of their own accord, be it autoerotic or otherwise, is widely seen as an aberration, a gross perversion of the clear line we have drawn from childhood sexual purity to the overpowering sexual urges we've convinced ourselves arrive, apparently out of nowhere, at the onset of adolescence.

In his essay "Der Erlkönig: The Ambiguities of Horror," film theorist Robin Wood points out that much of Western culture mistakes innocence for the absence of sexual desire, thereby converting true innocence into a "false, desexualized innocence" and demanding that we repress anything resembling sexual desire until it is deemed appropriate or natural by society. To admit sexuality in children doesn't merely force us to reimagine what sexuality actually is—it works against the cherished myth that childhood is a blissful time free of some of the more complicated aspects of being alive: anger, pain, boredom, disappointment, rejection, anxiety, fear, loneliness, guilt, and sexual desire. This "forced asexuality," as Shulamith Firestone calls it, is but one way adults tend to diminish the humanity and complexity of youth.

I once attended a lecture by an unimportant white male novelist who encouraged aspiring writers to return to the feral state of childhood innocence and wonderment when writing. He conjured a youth spent running naked through muddy New England woods and basking in the dizzying warmth of his apron-wearing mother's love. After the lecture, I asked the novelist what a writer should do if their childhood didn't necessarily resemble his romantic vision. He nodded kindly, his eyes brimming with palpable sympathy. "I'm so sorry," he said, "for everything you went through."

I was taken aback. I'd been attempting to point out, as politely and unconfrontationally as possible, that not every person grows up in New England with an apron-wearing, stay-at-home mother. For many, childhood is a tumultuous time of confusion, frustration, and hurt, and significant numbers of children, especially children who aren't white, are often excluded from such sentimental fantasies of innocence and unencumbered joy. Though I wasn't necessarily talking about my own childhood, which had been for the most part absurdly privileged and happy, it was clear he assumed I was demurely referencing some personal experience of horrendous childhood abuse and neglect.

The exchange stuck with me long after I'd filed out of the lecture hall. In so much of the American imagination, I realized, children are either senselessly happy little sprites traipsing through life without a care or the helpless victims of unimaginable cruelty and horror, forever hobbled by the tragedy of their joyless youth.

For a brief moment in the 1960s and '70s, activists attempted to challenge and expand this limited view of childhood. The children's rights movements marks a vibrant but mostly forgotten attempt to restore agency and independence to young people, whom advocates considered yet another repressed class suffering under the suffocating regime of the patriarchal nuclear family. Children's liberation was directly tied to both women's liberation and the gay rights movement. Many gay rights activists believed that expanding societal definitions around family and sexuality also meant expanding our definition of childhood. Radical feminists like Shulamith Firestone and Kate Millett argued that women would never experience true freedom and equality as long as children remained dependent on them emotionally, physically, and economically for so much of their lives. In *The Dialectic of Sex,* Firestone calls both childhood and femininity "mutually reinforcing oppressions" so intertwined that "we will be unable to speak of the liberation of women without also discussing the liberation of children, and vice versa." Shulamith argued that the birth of the nuclear family and the accompanying reinvention of children as a separate class to be coddled and surveilled stalled the once-rapid progression from infancy to maturity, saddling women with the duties of childrearing for decades.

Though much of the children's rights movement involved pushing for relatively palatable reforms such as community day care and expanding the definition of "family" to include gay couples and their children, certain groups also pushed for an end to the puritanical policing of all forms of sexuality, including that of children. Various advocates scandalized the public by arguing that parents should not deprive their children of what Kate Millett called "the great power of auto-eroticism." Millett claimed that by denying or punishing early signs of sexuality in children, we risk "poisoning [their sexuality]" for the rest of their lives. She writes, "The guilt and shame imposed upon on us as adults, though first imposed upon us as children, is imposed on us again as we reimpose it upon a new generation, perpetuating the sins of the past and its conception of sin." Though many of these arguments weren't all that different from those of Freud, who had long ago asserted that infants are infinitely sexual beings, they were threatening because they were adamantly political, subversively wrapped up in the ideologies of women's liberation, gay rights, and the sexual revolution. Acknowledging sexuality in children was only slightly more threatening than acknowledging sexuality in women or accepting the sexualities of gay men and women as meaningful and valid. At the time, physician and public health activist Mary S. Calderone wrote that acknowledging sexuality in children was as controversial and necessary as Galileo confirming that the earth revolved around the sun.

The children's rights movement ultimately stalled out for many reasons. People were understandably turned off by some of its more morally ambiguous proscriptions, such as permitting intergenerational sex. Others worried the children's rights movement actually risked rolling back important gains made for vulnerable young people over the course of the twentieth century. Were six-year-olds supposed to go back to the factories and mines just so their mothers could feel free? By the 1980s and '90s, the surging moral panic around child kidnapping, abuse, and molestation reached such a fever pitch that it was nearly impossible to imagine children, namely white children, as anything other than a sweet and endangered species that must be protected from the limitless dangers of the outside world at all costs.

If anyone wanted evidence of the dangers of acknowledging childhood sexuality, they needed only point to *The Exorcist,* with its brutal depiction of desire gone berserk, to show what might happen to the nation's pure and hearty youth if we allowed them to succumb to such perverse sexual urges. In *Minor Feelings: An Asian American Reckoning,* Cathy Park Hong critiques American filmmakers like Wes Anderson and Steven Spielberg who create charming and carefully curated odes to the wonders of white childhood, artfully excluding any racial or historical context that might cloud their sentimental visions. Hong describes Hollywood as the "most reactionary cultural perpetrator of white nostalgia, stuck in a time loop and refusing to acknowledge that America's racial demographics have radically changed since 1965."

The Exorcist can be seen as the terrifying inverse of films like *E.T.* or *Moonrise Kingdom.* It is still obsessed with some falsified notion of innocence, but rather than fetishizing its purity, it revels in its bloody degradation.

•

Despite Friedkin's colorful story about Linda Blair's audition for *The Exorcist,* Blair has maintained that she did not know what masturbation was when she was cast, nor did she understand what was happening in this scene when it was filmed. In the documentary *The Fear of God: 25 Years of The Exorcist,* Blair says, "A child does not know what those words mean. . . . A child does not understand what masturbation is." Blair describes shooting the scene as "very mechanical," with Friedkin carefully directing her every move.

To counter the media storm claiming that Blair was psychologically disturbed by the intensity of her role, Friedkin and Blatty have always maintained that production was a fun and lighthearted affair for their young star. You can find photographs and footage online of Linda Blair laughing and smiling on the set, drinking milkshakes in her hospital gown and goofing off for the camera while bound to the bed. Friedkin even says he became a "surrogate father" to Blair, tickling her playfully before shooting particularly gruesome scenes and taking the time to explain things like lens types and lighting to her during moments of downtime. By most accounts, Blair was an incredibly bright and well-adjusted young girl, a "jewel," according to Blatty, who never once complained about anything.

Blair, once again, counters this narrative.

"I don't think anyone has ever understood how hard it was on my end," she has said of filming *The Exorcist.* From Blair's perspective, it wasn't that she never complained. It was that she did complain, but no one heard or understood.

Most famously, Blair was injured while filming a scene where her out-of-control body flails and thrashes on the bed, jerking up and down like a jackknife. To shoot the scene, Marcel Vercoutere, the notorious French special effects coordinator, strapped Blair into a remote-controlled harness that he operated with relish from the sidelines. In 1983 Vercoutere told *Fangoria* magazine,

I was the devil! . . . I had her strapped in there, and I was throwing her back and forth. . . . When does the acting start and the realism begin? To say she is being possessed and thrown and picked up, jiggled and bumped, and to get that horror and not going too far, not to hurt her, or bruise her. Up to a certain point, it's for fun, then it starts to get more violent. And she starts to say, "Okay I've had enough." Now that's when you start!

Blair had no control over when the contraption stopped or started, or how fast her own body was made to move. Not surprisingly, she ended up injuring her back when a piece of the equipment came loose while filming.

"I'm supposed to be yelling, 'Make it stop!'" Blair told Mark Kermode. "And that's what I was yelling. But nobody realized I meant it."

The crew brought in doctors and a masseuse to treat her injury.

"A child's body will heal," Blair said. "And I was very strong. But it was tough work."[1]

To produce the vomit that Regan must spew over the priests, master makeup artist Dick Smith devised a plastic mouth harness, not unlike a horse's bit, which would pump pea soup into Blair's mouth through a nozzle. Blair describes spending hours on set with her mouth wide open.

Though Blair's body double, Eileen Dietz, has since claimed that she was actually the one forced to wear the bit, Blair nonetheless endured a string of equal discomforts at the hands of

---

1. Ellen Burstyn also injured her back on a Vercoutere-designed contraption that yanked her across the unpadded floor during the masturbation scene, leaving her in crutches for the rest of production. Friedkin has denied that Burstyn was seriously harmed.

Smith and the production crew. The contacts she wore to turn her eyeballs white reportedly stung, and the glue used to secure prosthetic scars to her face burned and irritated her skin. For the possession scenes, when Friedkin kept the set at frigid temperatures, the crew wore old ski suits to keep warm. Blair, on the other hand, spent most of the day in a thin nightgown and long underwear, shivering and blue lipped, even as snow reportedly fell around her.

Actresses often describe the hours they spend in the makeup chair as a kind of excruciating and mind-numbing endurance test. Blair is no different, except that she did her time staring not only at her own transformation but also at the reflection of the grotesque Regan dummy used in the scene where her head does a 360, which Dick Smith insisted on keeping in her dressing room.

Of being forced to stare at her shadow-demon self for hours on end, Blair has said, "I didn't enjoy the experience of being in its presence."

•

Though Friedkin has stated over the years that Blair had no stand-in or substitute, it has since been officially acknowledged that snippets of the more graphic scenes were actually performed by a body double, Eileen Dietz. In the case of the crucifix masturbation, it is Dietz's hands we see driving the blood-splattered crucifix into her crotch, not Blair's. Dietz appears on and off again throughout the rest of the film, for a total of twenty-eight and a half seconds. Warner Bros. was forced to do the calculation when Dietz, along with Mercedes McCambridge, sued for credit. Unlike McCambridge, who simply wanted credit for voicing Pazuzu, Dietz falsely claimed to have performed *all* of the possession sequences in the film.

The ensuing public battle between Dietz and Blair was nick-named "the Great Pea Soup War."[2]

Though the knowledge that young Blair was not in fact miming masturbation did little to stem rumors that she was psychologically deranged by the role (the world, it seemed, really did want her to be broken by it), some believe it did hurt her chances of winning Best Supporting Actress at the 1974 Academy Awards. The Oscar instead went to another child actress, the plucky eleven-year-old Tatum O'Neal, who starred alongside her real-life father in Peter Bogdanovich's black-and-white period piece, *Paper Moon.*

Blair didn't win the Academy Award, but she did announce the award for Best Short Subject alongside actor Billy Dee Williams, who had recently won praise for his performance in the Billie Holiday biopic, *Lady Sings the Blues.* On stage, Williams asked Blair if she'd gotten around to watching her much-talked-about performance in *The Exorcist.* Blair cocked her head and smiled, preparing for one of those inescapable Oscars one-liners.

"Well," she replied sagely, "I don't like standing in lines."

Though O'Neal made history that year as the youngest person ever to win an Academy Award, perhaps Blair deserves credit for a different Hollywood first. Hedy Lamarr may have performed the first on-screen orgasm in the film *Ekstase,* but Linda Blair will forever be marked by cinematic masturbation's

2. Confusion remains about who exactly performed the famous spider-walk scene in *The Exorcist.* In Mark Kermode's book on *The Exorcist,* he claims that the spider walk was performed by a stunt-woman named Linda R. Hager with the help of wires and a harness designed by Vercoutere. However, after the sensational rerelease of the film in 2000, a stuntwoman by the name of Ann Miles came forward to claim that she was the one who actually performed the infamous scene. Hager has since released a notarized statement confirming she did not perform the scene, and the consensus seems to be that Miles, not Hager or Dietz or Blair, does indeed deserve credit for the spider walk.

opening salvo, the sound of something sacred and sharp tearing through young female flesh.

•

Among feminist film critics, the crucifix-masturbation scene in *The Exorcist* is by far the most discussed, analyzed, and reviled of the entire film. It isn't hard to see why. I can think of few other moments in cinema history that so brutally exemplify the male fear of female sexuality. *The Exorcist* takes a young girl's entry into adolescence and twists it into something perverted and evil. Whatever pleasure Regan might indeed be taking in her own sexual awakening is sidelined by the sheer visual horror of her ravenous demonic display. By the film's logic, to be a young woman filled with sexual desire is to be possessed by a corrupt and unforgiving force. It is to transform into something out of control, dangerous, and unrecognizable. Part of me wonders if this is what my mother was trying to protect me from when she banned me from seeing *The Exorcist* as a child: the powerful lies the film told me about who I was and who I would become.

Throughout her possession, Regan's voice deepens to a masculine, oddly British-inflected baritone (thanks, of course, to the iconic vocal performance of McCambridge, a woman forty-three years Blair's senior.) Her language becomes increasingly filthy and ridiculous. Her face and body mutate almost beyond recognition: her skin turns ghostly pale, slashed with deep and oozing cuts, and her teeth are clearly rotting in her skull. When she opens her mouth, her breath is so foul that everyone around her puts their sleeves to their noses. She is no longer Regan. She is a putrid and volatile thing.

The film, of course, makes no effort to portray Regan as human. We never once step inside Regan's head or see the experience from her perspective. Regan terrifies us because her mind, emotions, and experience of her body remain an utter mystery. As Carol J. Clover notes in *Men, Women, and Chain Saws: Gender in the Modern Horror Film,* the primary focus of *The Exorcist* is not so much Regan as it is the transformation that Regan's hysterical body prompts in the fragile male psyche. Clover writes,

> Unlike the male story, which for all its variation is an essentially coherent change of heart, the female story ricochets from extreme to extreme, flailing as narrative and as system of sympathies in much the same way that the woman herself flails as character. . . . Especially in possession films, moderate slides into explosive; appealingly open becomes monstrously open; emotionally impressionable becomes mentally ill; charmingly pregnant becomes hideously pregnant, and so on. . . . To make matters worse, although some of the stories peak there, others go a step further and have the woman become so colonized she virtually becomes her possessor.

Regan is pure spectacle, there to frighten the audience into submission and hurry the plot toward a satisfying conclusion, one which, of course, is brought about by the heroic actions of the male priests.

Consciously or not, the film forcefully asserts that women who defy sexual and behavioral norms—women who dare to be angry, assertive, and sexual—must be shamed, punished, and controlled back into passive and caring submission. Critic Andrew Britton writes, "We are allowed Regan's subversion of ideology, but in a form so inherently monstrous as to preconclude that the restoration of the ideology (read as normalcy) is necessary." In its utter horror, *The Exorcist* forecloses any potential for real subversion. Regan's sexuality and rage are portrayed as so violent and unnatural that their end can only come as a blessed relief. In the film's final scene, when Regan has returned to her prior status as demure and wide-eyed young innocent, unable to remember any of the things she said and did while possessed, we are meant to sigh in gratitude.

But what to make of the possibility that Regan isn't actually masturbating at all?

In the novel, Blatty writes the scene as a kind of battle between the devil, who is forcing Regan to stab herself with the "bone-white crucifix," and Regan herself, who is terrified by what the devil is trying to make her do. "Oh, please! Oh no, *please!*" she shrieks as she strains to push the crucifix away from her splayed legs. Ultimately, however, the force of the devil is too powerful, and, in a terrifying moment of super-natural rape, Regan relents, "[thrusting] down the crucifix into her vagina and [beginning] to masturbate ferociously, roaring in that deep, coarse, deafening voice."

"Masturbating with a crucifix" has generally been how the culture has described the infamous scene in the decades since the film's premier, as I've done here. Regan barking "Let Jesus fuck you" lends undeniably sexual and sacrilegious overtones to the scene, and it is hard *not* to view something that involves female genitals and anything even vaguely phallic as sexual, plain and simple.

Viewed without any preconceived notions of what the scene actually is, however, I think it looks far closer to a moment of radical self-harm than a scene of demonic self-pleasure, an act of desperate mutilation and subjugation, the product of a culture so hateful and twisted that a young girl doesn't know how to do anything but tear herself apart, even when she is alone.

•

One of the strangest things about having been an adolescent female in America is that humiliating and dehumanizing things happened to me so constantly and so casually that I have forgotten most of them completely. In fact, the only way I am able to remember some of the more undignified things I went through as a teenager is by reading my journals, which I kept religiously from the age of fourteen to the age of twenty-eight.

The journal from my junior year in high school is particularly illustrative. I spend most of its pages bemoaning the size of my thighs and the lackluster flicker of my personality. Large chunks of it are devoted to cataloging everything I ate that day and complaining about my "pimple brow," which I define as a kind of unsightly unibrow made of zits. Junior year was also the year I became obsessed with a redheaded boy named Aidan who played the acoustic guitar, ran cross country, and sat behind me in AP English. I liked how Aidan would spend class gently stroking the faux fur on the hood of my jacket while whispering *"shhhh,"* as if comforting a small woodland animal. We hung out together often but never officially dated, never even kissed. The closest we ever got to sexual contact was on the night of Winter Formal, which I vividly recounted in my journal.

Instead of going to the dance like most other students, my grade-school friend Nicole Smith and I went over to the house of a boy named Ryan to play *Rock Band* in his attic with Aidan and our other friend, Anthony. We spent an hour or so boisterously recreating "Creep" and "Wave of Mutilation" in front of the TV before growing bored and walking to the nearest grocery store with the vague notion of finding someone to buy us beer. When that failed, we returned to Ryan's house and hunkered down on his big leather couch to watch the new

James Bond movie, *Casino Royale,* on DVD. In the entry, I am careful to point out the exact configuration of our bodies on the couch: Aidan, Nicole, Ryan, me, Anthony. Two girls sandwiched between three boys.

Shortly after a scene in which Bond gropes a busty Italian woman on a shadowy hotel room floor, Anthony turned to me and began to, as I flippantly describe it in my journal, "fondle my boobs." I don't bother mentioning what I thought or felt as he did so, only that, "after much struggle," I leapt from the couch and, "freed myself from the torturous situation."

As I stood in the center of the room in front of the flashing TV, the three boys stood up, encircled me, and began taking turns lunging at my chest. Ryan grabbed my chest and pushed me over to Anthony, who grabbed my chest and pushed me over to Aidan, who grabbed my chest, declared my breasts "supple," and then pushed me back to Ryan. I giggled and flailed about for several rounds of what was clearly, to them, a game, until I somewhat deliriously began shrieking, "Stop, stop!" Though my shirt stayed on, they yanked it down so far that my padded, hot-pink AA Victoria's Secret bra was fully visible. Nicole watched from the couch, embalmed in a blanket, saying nothing.

After it ended, I did not cry or run away. I sat back down with them, and I finished the movie. In the journal entry, I describe the night as "fun."

Up until I reread the entry, I recalled everything about the night *except* this rather brief but shocking incident. I remembered the cool chill in the air as the five of us dashed across Beaverton-Hillsdale Highway to the Fred Meyer, and I remembered watching Daniel Craig scale cranes and sprint through a construction site in the heat-warped streets of Madagascar. I remember my annoyance that Nicole got to sit next to Aidan on the couch.

Once I read the entry, however, the strange memory of it came instantly flooding back. I could hear the sound of my deranged, almost drugged laughter as I let my body go limp and flop from one open-palmed boy to the next, and I could recall feeling complimented to be in the center of it all because it meant, much to my exhilaration, that they all wanted *me*. When Aidan called my breasts "supple," I remember feeling a surge of pure joy.

I am less shocked that something like this happened to me than I am by the fact that it happened and I completely forgot about it until well over a decade later. After I read this entry, I couldn't help but think of Christine Blasey Ford's testimony before the Senate Judiciary Committee in October 2018, describing her decades-old sexual assault at the hands of Trump-appointed Supreme Court Justice Brett Kavanaugh and his friends, not because I think the two incidents are the same but because I find their differences illuminating.

Unlike in Ford's case, none of us, despite our half-hearted attempts, were drunk. I wasn't scared the boys would rape or kill me, and the incident didn't "haunt me episodically" for years to come. I harbor no real resentment toward these boys or any desire to shame them publicly (I've changed their names here). In fact, I kept silent not because I was "afraid and ashamed to tell anyone the details" but because I forgot about it, or maybe because I didn't deem it important enough to remember, or maybe because it was easier to dismiss the humiliating memory than to integrate it into my daily life and sense of self. The night didn't "alter my life" in any way I can consciously recall. Rather, I shrugged off the mundane degradation and let it bleed imperceptibly into all the other ways I was learning to see myself as an object and design my self-respect in relation to men and become complicit almost daily in my own subjugation. By this point, I was so alienated from my body and its hungers that I took this quasi-attack as a kind of pleasure.

Ford was especially powerful when evoking the stark differences between how deeply the incident scarred her and how little it seemed to have affected Kavanaugh. At the hearing, when Kavanaugh blubbered like a fool and claimed to have no memory of what Ford was accusing him of, it made sense. Of course the night made no impression on him. It was a non-event. It was "fun."

Famously, Ford described the memory of hearing Kavanaugh's laughter as he nearly suffocated her in the dark bedroom. "Indelible," she called it.

What disturbed me most when I stumbled upon a vaguely similar incident from my own past was that *I* was the one who didn't remember it, and it is not my so-called assaulters' laughter that echoes in my ears years later, but my own.

Eventually, I know now, patriarchy teaches us all to twist its sharp blade ourselves.

•

The Exorcist turned Linda Blair into a major media figure, forever barraged by endless questions about what the film did to her impressionable young psyche. Blair's smiling child's face regularly appeared in the tabloids in those days, an uncanny actualization of the moment in *The Exorcist* when Regan's face appears on a magazine cover alongside her famous mother. One British tabloid showed a picture of Blair posing in a flower garden under the headline "The Devil Girl in the Daffodils."

In a promotional bit for *The Exorcist* filmed in London in 1973, the narrating journalist excuses his own mention of the subject by saying, "What she did in the film was repulsive and grotesque and the world wanted to be reassured that despite it all she was still an angel-faced all-American beauty." In the clip, Blair rides a horse through a park, looking confident and at peace despite the chaos that surrounds her. The narrator adds that Blair "sincerely believes she hasn't been scarred by any of the things she had to do in the film. . . . It's the grizzly business of stardom which seems more likely to permanently disfigure her."

From the moment *The Exorcist* premiered, Linda and her family were hounded by the press and began receiving death threats from both crazed fans and offended religious zealots. The studio hired bodyguards to live with the Blair family 24-7 for six months during the film's publicity circuit. Once the promotion for the movie ended, however, the studio decided they were no longer obligated to pay for the protection of the young star and promptly withdrew their services.

In a testament to just how slim the public's grip on reality is, people struggled to distinguish the difference between Linda the actress and the character she played in *The Exorcist*. Blair has said that people would often approach her on the streets genuinely terrified, accusing her of being a Satanist or sometimes even asking her to make her head spin around. In the public imagination, Linda and Regan fused. Friedkin had deliberately blurred the line between fact and fiction, between monster and girl, and Linda arguably became the chief victim of *The Exorcist*'s ever-enduring mythology.

Linda would never become the child who starred in movies about horses, about young girls and their dogs. Instead, she landed roles in stories about helpless young victims and depraved fallen women. In September 1974, Blair returned to the screen, albeit a smaller one, in the made-for-TV movie *Born Innocent,* about a fourteen-year-old girl named Chris who suffers extreme physical, psychological, and sexual abuse throughout her childhood and eventually winds up in a juvenile detention center. The film made history for featuring the first all-female rape scene, in which a group of girls surrounds Chris in the shower and violently rapes her using a plunger handle. The scene ends with the naked Blair crying on the bathroom floor. The previews for the movie show salacious snippets from the scene while an announcer says in voice-over, "She was born innocent, but that was fourteen years ago!" The scene, like her masturbation scene the year before, caused a public outcry, kick-starting the first of the many scandals of Linda's career.

The movie stoked controversy before it even premiered. Advertisers began pulling their sponsorships, and NBC aired an advisory message warning that the film's "realistic and forthright" content should not be "viewed by young people or others in their family who might be disturbed by it." Many families ended up tuning in regardless, likely mistaking it for another NBC film set to air around the same time, *Born Wild*, about wildlife conservation in Africa. A promotional spread in the *New York Times* featured *Born Innocent* and *Born Wild* side by side, Linda Blair's famous young face appearing alongside that of a roaring lioness. In *Wallowing in Sex: The New Sexual Culture of 1970s American Television,* Elana Levine writes, "Because Blair's work in *The Exorcist* already led to associations between her and out-of-control (possessed) sexuality, the doubling of Blair's image with a wild animal further enhanced the suggestion of forbidden, sex-tinged danger."

Gay, lesbian, and women's rights activists and critics vehemently decried the rape scene. The group Feminist Lesbian Liberation called it "propaganda against lesbianism." Many also believed the brutal plunger rape scene also contributed to the real-life assault of a nine-year-old girl who was, according to the *Washington Post*, "artificially raped" with a soda bottle on a San Francisco beach by her peers: three girls and a boy ranging in age from ten to fifteen. At trial, the victim's lawyer argued that *Born Innocent* stimulated violent and antisocial conduct through the graphic, repetitive, and exceptionally long nature of the rape scene, in which the plunger is repeatedly thrust into Blair over the course of two and a quarter minutes.

The controversy surrounding the film led the National Association of Broadcasters to implement a Family Viewing Hour, but the California Supreme Court eventually ruled that NBC was not liable for the attack or what the *Washington Post* called "the harm inflicted on a child that was born and was still innocent."

•

Blair landed similar roles in the years that followed—*Sweet Hostage* and *Sarah T.: Portrait of a Teenage Alcoholic*—before eventually returning to the big screen in 1977 for the disastrous *Exorcist* sequel, *Exorcist II: The Heretic*.[3] In the film, Regan is now a busty teenager with potential telepathic abilities attending a state-of-the-art psychiatric institute led by a woman named Dr. Gene Tuskin (played by Louise Fletcher, of Nurse Ratched fame), who is helping her recover from her demonic possession four years before. Though Regan claims she remembers nothing of her possession beyond "being very sick and having nightmares," Tuskin argues that she has merely repressed those memories in order to avoid reckoning with her own trauma as well as the pain and turmoil she caused while possessed. "We make our own demons up here!" Tuskin insists, pointing to her head.

To access these repressed memories, Dr. Tuskin connects with Regan's brainwaves via a state-of-the-art "biofeedback"

---

3. Neither Friedkin nor Blatty had any involvement in the sequel, though Blatty returned to write and direct *The Exorcist III*.

device that allows her to travel into the deep reaches of Regan's addled mind. In order to "synch," as they call it, the participants attach electrodes to their heads and stare deep into a strobe light. When I watched the movie with my brother, he called it "some Christopher Nolan shit." Through the machine, they enter a "deep state of hypnosis" that will allow them to "understand and dissolve" the painful memories of Regan's past.

Exorcist II: The Heretic is undeniably a horrible film, but there is something oddly refreshing about it. In it, we see Regan as a fuller character. She speaks, she interacts with other people, she leaves her room and explores the world. And in the end, Regan is revealed to be the most powerful character of all.

This power remained mostly a fantasy. In the following years, Blair's life continued to be shaped primarily by the harsh glare of public attention. At times, Linda seemed to enjoy her strange breed of fame, dating teen heartthrob Rick Spring field and hanging out with superstars like Steven Tyler, Keith Moon, and Linda Lovelace. In 1977, the same year *Exorcist II* premiered, Linda was embroiled in a drug scandal involving a quarter ounce of cocaine, the daughter of a Florida senator, and a pedigree puppy. Blair eventually pled guilty to federal misdemeanor charges and was fined $5,000, put on three years of probation, and instructed to give twelve public anti-drug appearances, likely prompting more than one kid to tell his friends, "The chick from *The Exorcist* just told me not to smoke pot!"

She spent the late '70s and '80s starring in a series of highly sexualized B movies: the musical *Roller Boogie,* the slasher/haunted house flick *Hell Night,* and the German-American prison exploitation picture *Chained Heat,* the poster of which advertised, "What these women did to get into prison is nothing compared to what they'll do to get out." Blair was nominated for Worst Actress at the Golden Raspberry Awards five times, her Academy Award chances long forgotten. Linda also posed for several adult magazines during these years, including the cover of Italian *Playboy*, where her voluptuous breasts spill out of a bright blue corset, and the French soft-porn magazine *Oui*, where she wears aviators and excitedly clutches her chest.

Blair eventually traded Rick Springfield in for Rick James. Rick has stated that Linda wasn't the inspiration for his mega-hit "Super Freak," but she was the inspiration for his other, less famous song, "Cold Blooded," in which he sings, "Girl, I think you're so sexy, sexy, sexy / cold blooded." With a few clicks you can find intimate photos of the couple online. I'm not sure how or when these photos became publicly available, but I'd guess it was the work of some guileless journalist or attention seeker scavenging Blair's most private and vulnerable moments for further evidence that the Devil Girl was hopelessly depraved.

In one photo, the two of them pose together in bed, James's long hair cascading down his shoulders in braids, Linda looking at the camera with her characteristically round and smiling face. In another, Linda's shirtless chest is pressed up against James's as she turns toward the camera, her head, unlike the demon dummy she'd been forced to stare at all those years before, only managing a mere 180.

•

Over the years, it seems Blair has made peace with her status as horror icon. Now, fifty years after the film's premiere, Blair is an unmarried vegan who runs a charity for abused and abandoned animals outside of her home in Orange County, California. If Hollywood wouldn't let her star in movies about little girls and their dogs, then she would just have to become that little girl herself, half a century too late. Linda, it seems, feels an intense connection to the pit bull, a creature forever stalked by its own cultural misrepresentations and media-fueled hysterias.

Blair remains a modest public figure, occasionally signing T-shirts at horror conventions or hosting reality TV shows like *Scariest Places on Earth*, where she takes armchair ghost hunters inside places haunted by their pasts: sanitoriums, plantations, prisons. In 2006 she told the *New York Daily News*, "I think I have been extremely polite about answering questions about *The Exorcist* almost every day of my life."

In 2014 she appeared as a guest judge on *RuPaul's Drag Race*. She seems genuinely excited to be there. "I can't believe you're here," RuPaul jokes. "My head is spinning!" Her fellow judge, Michelle Visage, is wearing a pair of diamond-studded crucifix earrings, and one of the contestants, BenDeLaCreme, makes the obligatory joke.

It seems oddly fitting that Blair would appear on a TV show like *RuPaul's Drag Race*, where the florid extremes of her performance in *The Exorcist* could be celebrated instead of mocked and shamed. Fitting, too, that the episode is titled "Scream Queens," in reference to the female horror actresses who may never have garnered mainstream success outside of the genre but are nonetheless worshiped and respected by their legions of fans. Just as the "final girl" trope has been reclaimed and reappraised in the years since the publication of Carol J. Clover's *Men, Women, and Chain Saws*, so too might we begin to see all the problems and extremes of the possession film in a new light.

Does the masturbation scene from *The Exorcist* have radical potential? After all, to acknowledge female and/or childhood sexuality on the screen at all in 1973, however monstrous, is, in its own demented way, a kind of progress. In "An Introduction to the American Horror Film," Robin Wood writes, "Central to the effect and fascination of horror films is their fulfillment of our nightmare wish to smash the norms that oppress us and that our moral conditioning teaches us to revere." I've watched Regan drive the bloody crucifix deep inside of her many times, and each time, I find myself desperately searching for the subversive. Is it possible to read this scene as a sly cinematic critique of patriarchy's deep-seated fear and loathing of both female sexuality and rage? Or perhaps as a taboo-busting demolition of Catholicism's empty symbols and repressive sexual norms? Does the film, through sheer visual might, force viewers to accept the imperfect reality of female sexual desire and in doing so also raise the possibility that women can pursue and fulfill that desire entirely without men? Does *The Exorcist* gleefully warp the hallowed coming-of-age tale and in doing so present a truer representation of the horrors of growing up female in America? Is Regan the ultimate emancipated woman, free to be ugly and foul-mouthed and horny and mean in the most graphically sacrilegious ways possible?

I want to reclaim the scene for Linda and for myself and for my mother and for all the other young girls and women forced to grow up in its brutal wake, but I'm not sure it is possible. As I write this, I find myself thinking about a Maggie Nelson quote from *The Argonauts*. Nelson is talking about discovering *I Know Why the Caged Bird Sings* as a little girl and constantly rereading Angelou's "primal scene of violation," in which Angelou describes her sexual abuse by Mr. Freeman. Nelson writes, "If you're looking for sexual tidbits as a female child, and the only ones that present themselves depict child rape or other violations, then your sexuality will form around that fact. There is no control group. I don't even want to talk about 'female sexuality' until there is a control group. And there never will be."

It is especially difficult to talk about your sexuality as a woman because you don't know what is your own and what has been unfairly thrust upon you by the outside world. The Nelson quote speaks to how cultural narratives and representations distort your own self-perception and influence the most intimate and tender parts of your inner life in ways you often cannot fully articulate or control. Of course, things are changing. More than ever before, women are free to create honest art and show female sexuality in a plurality of ways: as something ecstatic, comic, carefree, confusing, complicated. I am especially grateful for *Fleabag* and *Broad City,* shows that embrace masturbation as a goofy and unremarkable part of a woman's life.

Still, I don't think we will ever understand "female sexuality" until we live in a world cleansed of the kind of images like the ones we see in *The Exorcist.* Considering how deeply embedded those images are in our national psyche, it seems delusional to think we will reach that place any time soon, if ever. Even if we eliminate them, we are unlikely to forget them, and even if we forget them, they'll still be there somewhere, the whetted point of their violence slashing at us in our sleep.

JAMES BALDWIN SEES
THE EXORCIST IN 1973

James Baldwin went to see *The Exorcist* twice when it premiered in the winter of 1973, first with a friend and then later by himself. He saw it in Hollywood, a place he'd traveled to five years before to write the screenplay for *The Autobiography of Malcom X,* a film that would linger in cinematic purgatory until Spike Lee made *Malcolm X* over two decades later. Baldwin's ill-fated foray into the movie industry, which he would later refer to as "my Hollywood sentence," had left him bitter and discouraged. Still, he entered the darkened theater that December with an open mind, summoning his boyhood self who once believed in the devil and the Holy Ghost.

Baldwin's willingness to see the film was part anthropological. Since his youthful days of going to the movies with his beloved schoolteacher, Ms. Miller, he had seen film as a way of answering a question that perpetually nagged him: "What, under the heavens or beneath the sea or in the catacombs of hell, would cause any people to act the way white people acted?" *The Exorcist,* a massive cultural event that left filmgoers vomiting, fainting, and running out of the theaters in a panic, must have seemed like particularly fertile cinematic terrain. You didn't just go to the theater to watch the movie. You went to watch the audience too.

After seeing the film for the first time, Baldwin and his friend David got drinks at a nearby bar. It is in a bar that Father Karras, the young priest in the film, first admits to his friend Father Tom that he may have lost his faith, and so it is only fitting that in a bar David expressed his own fascination with Karras's struggles.

"We must be careful," David told Baldwin, "lest we lose our faith—and become possessed."

Baldwin sensed that his friend was no longer talking about the film, or about the church.

Later, when Baldwin saw *The Exorcist* alone, he studied his fellow moviegoers closely, watching as they raced down the aisles and out the swinging theater doors, their shocked eyes turned away from the screen in panic. He writes, "I wondered what they were seeing, and what it meant to them." I imagine Baldwin sitting slouched and contemplative in some popcorn-strewn Los Angeles theater, hand cradling his chin and feet propped up on the seat in front of him as he ponders why, in America, a country long practiced in cruelty and hate, people were suddenly so terrified of a twelve-year-old little girl.

Two years later, when Baldwin finally sat down to write about *The Exorcist* and other films for his book *The Devil Finds Work,* he could barely contain his disdain.

"*The Exorcist,*" he writes, "has absolutely nothing going for it, except Satan, who is certainly the star: I can say only that Satan was never like this when he crossed my path. . . . His concerns were far more various, and his methods more subtle."

To Baldwin, the film reeked of a particularly resilient strain of white American obliviousness and greed. Baldwin reserved special criticism for Chris, a so-called "liberated woman" who, in his view, seeks out an exorcism not to save her writhing daughter's soul but rather to ensure she grows up to be a wealthy and complacent white woman just like herself. In Baldwin's view, Chris isn't so much terrified that her daughter has transformed into a cruel and violent monster as she is concerned that her possessed daughter's shocking behavior—the swearing, the crudeness, the disdain for authority, the overt sexuality—makes her unpalatable to the stratum of white society that Chris, a successful woman who gets invited to the White House for dinner, so comfortably occupies.

Indeed, Baldwin saw none of the overt and transformative spirituality that novelist, screenwriter, and producer William Peter Blatty envisioned for the story after he'd first read about the possession of a young white boy in the *Washington Post* years before. Baldwin writes, "*The Exorcist* is not in the least concerned with damnation, an abysm far beyond the confines of its imagination, but with property, with safety, tax shelters, stocks and bonds, rising and falling markets, the continued invulnerability of a certain class of people, and the continued sanctification of a certain history."

All of which is just another way of saying: the mechanisms that keep white supremacy in place.

•

Like so much of the horror genre up until fairly recently, *The Exorcist* is a very white film. Every main character in the film is white, as are most secondary and tertiary characters. Other than the Black nurses at Regan's doctor's office and at the state hospital, the only time people of color appear on screen is in the background, when Father Karras visits his ailing mother in a tenement in graffiti-covered Manhattan. A group of teenage boys—Black and Puerto Rican, it seems—play and shout on the streets as Karras enters his mother's decaying building. A viewer could miss them, I suppose, but their presence feels intentional, meant to cue viewers to the fact that Karras's mother, a Greek immigrant, lives in a "bad" neighborhood, an "ethnic" one. Father Karras has left the safe confines of the Catholic Church and entered the dangerous urban jungle.

In the book version of *The Exorcist,* Blatty plays up this urban decay, describing a crumbling "hovel" of an apartment where the "dingy walls and soiled floors [seeped] into [Karras's] bones." The New York sequence, which also features an unsettling moment in which a blind homeless man in a subway tunnel reaches out to Karras, asking him to help "an old altar boy," stands in sharp contrast to the polished wealth and scholarly decorum of historic Georgetown, where the rest of the film is set. This was New York City in the 1970s after all, a city with a racially coded reputation as a crime-ridden cesspool where you were lucky if you stepped outside your door without getting mugged. However briefly and subtly, *The Exorcist*'s New York sequence panders to growing white fears around cities, violence, youth of color, and crime.

Richard Pryor mocked the extreme whiteness of *The Exorcist* in a stand-up bit in which he jokes that if the movie had had any leading Black characters, it "would have been about seven minutes long." He later parlayed this into a skit on *Saturday Night Live,* in which two Black priests, played by Pryor and Thalmus Rasulala (the actor who played Dr. Gordon Thomas in the Blaxploitation horror classic *Blacula*), visit the home of a white family to perform an exorcism on a possessed little girl. As soon as Pryor hears the demonic moans coming from the floor above, he immediately turns to leave.

"Where's your faith, father?" asks Rasulala.

"It's in the car," Pryor replies, backtracking. "I'm gonna go get it."

When the pair finally ventures upstairs, it only takes a few

TV-friendly demonic insults—for example, "Your mother eats kitty litter!"—before both the priests snap and start strangling the girl in her bed.

The spoof is funny and effective as comedy at the same time that it quietly hits upon a larger truth about the ways in which white cruelty is so often coddled and excused in the name of some historically disproven notion of white American goodness. Pryor and Rasulala see something all those white movie-goers had missed: Maybe Regan should have been slapped all along.

•

One year after *The Exorcist* premiered, the growing Blaxploitation industry took on demonic horror in the film *Abby*, which is about a young, Black, church-going wife in Kentucky who becomes possessed by a Yoruba sex demon. While possessed, Abby (played by Carol Speed) abandons her Christian decorum and gleefully seduces a series of men, only to kill them afterward.

In *Horror Noire: Blacks in the American Horror Film from the 1890s to Present,* Robin R. Means Coleman argues that Black actresses in horror films were not allowed to become triumphant final girls like Ripley in *Alien* or Laurie in *Halloween*—those asexual, slightly masculinized figures who beat back the murderous monsters using various phallic instruments of their choosing, no male savior necessary. Means Coleman argues that Black horror replaces the final girl with the "enduring woman" who stares down death only to face the ongoing threats of racism and sexism in the morning. Means Coleman writes, "In this regard, there is no going to sleep once the 'monster' is defeated, as the monster is often amorphously coded as 'Whitey,' and Whitey's oppressions are here to stay." Unfortunately, *Abby* is neither a final girl nor an enduring woman, as she is eventually saved from her murderous sexual life by her father-in-law, husband, and police officer brother, a plot that closely mirrors the male savior trajectory of *The Exorcist.*

Abby grossed a whopping $4 million in the month after its release. However, the film was quickly removed from theaters when Warner Bros. sued its distributor, American International Pictures, arguing that *Abby* was derivative of *The Exorcist.* In many ways, perhaps in most ways, it was. Down to the ancient demon unleashed on an archeological dig to its disaster-plagued production in Kentucky, the two films are incredibly similar. Director William Girdler, who helmed other Blaxploitation hits like *The Manitou* and *Grizzly* (itself considered a rip-off of *Jaws*), has even said, "Sure, we made *Abby* to come in on the shirttails of *The Exorcist.*" This, however, wasn't uncommon for Black horror films throughout the 1970s. Films like *Blacula, Blackenstein,* and *Dr. Black, Mr. Hyde* all shamelessly pilfered from white narratives in order to expose and critique the racism endemic to American society. What's more, *Abby* wasn't alone in taking inspiration from *The Exorcist.* Films in which good-hearted women are possessed by the devil or his demons proliferated after 1973 and continued to do so for decades, leaving one to wonder why Warner Bros. felt the need to single out *Abby* alone.

While numerous versions of *The Exorcist* are widely available for viewers to dissect and critique, *Abby* has virtually disappeared. Visually flawed copies of the film were rereleased in 2006 and 2007, including one advertised as "The Black Exorcist Edition," but the original print is not available to the public and the true "ownership" of the film remains unknown.

Seizing control of *Abby*'s distribution was another way Blaxploitation horror was boxed out of the box office despite its initial success, reestablishing horror as an inherently white genre reflecting inherently white fears and profitable only to white filmmakers. It would be decades before Black horror had a brief resurgence in the '90s and even longer before Jordan Peele's *Get Out* catapulted it back into the mainstream. *Get Out* proved to production studios that Black horror could be insanely popular and profitable, even as it contained a subversive message about racism and violence in America.

•

When it comes to race, *The Exorcist* trilogy is at best ambiguous and at worst deeply problematic. In *Exorcist II: The Heretic* and *The Exorcist III*, Black characters move out of the background and into the foreground in troubling and confusing ways. The prominent though vexing role race plays in the sequels may suggest that race was a larger occupation in the original *Exorcist* than is immediately apparent.

In *Exorcist II*, Father Lamont, a priest investigating Regan's original possession and the deaths that resulted from it, visits the institute where Regan is recovering. With the help of Dr. Tuskin, he uses the synching device to connect to Regan's brainwaves. While "inside" Regan's mind, Father Lamont is spirited away to Ethiopia by Pazuzu, the Mesopotamian wind demon that possessed Regan in the first film. There, he witnesses Father Merrin's past attempt to exorcise a demon from a boy named Kokumo while in a cave. These scenes, along with the opening sequence in which Father Lamont exorcises a demon from a writhing and growling Brazilian woman, situate the devil not in the body of a white American girl but in the bodies of the Black and Brown people living in the Southern Hemisphere. The rest of the plot isn't worth elaborating on, but it ends with Regan using a traditional African bullroarer instrument to banish Pazuzu from the earth while Lamont pulls a beating heart out of Regan's demonic doppelgänger.

The Exorcist III, released in 1990 and directed by William

Peter Blatty himself, opens with a Black boy running through the historic streets of Georgetown at night, hiding in shadowy corners and staring straight into the camera while holding out a bright red rose. He is wearing a shirt that says "Police Boys Club."

The scene is infuriating in its ambiguity. It feels menacing, but who is the threat? As viewers, are we supposed to be scared of the boy or something offscreen that is chasing the boy? The filmmaker seems to revel in this uncertainty, in what it might do to the people watching.

"It was like a demon," said the Ferguson police officer who killed Michael Brown when asked to describe Brown's face.

We soon learn that the little boy, Thomas Kintry, was recently murdered in what can only be described as a hate crime: decapitated and crucified on a pair of rowing oars, his head replaced with the head of a Jesus statue painted in blackface. Detective Kinderman, who investigated the murder of Burke Dennings in the first film, knows Thomas from the Police Boys Club, and he takes on the case.

Thomas's story is quickly pushed to the sidelines when Father Dyer, also a supporting character in the first film, is murdered in his hospital bed. The killer drained his blood supply and left it in jars by his bedside, not spilling a single drop. Before their murders, both Thomas Kintry and Father Dyer were injected with a paralytic that kept them wide awake throughout their entire painful deaths.

From here, the plot shifts focus to long conversations between Detective Kinderman and a convicted serial murderer nicknamed the Gemini Killer (who may or may not be the devil, who may or may not take the form of Father Karras). From inside a dank prison cell, Kinderman and the Gemini Killer share rambling, philosophical monologues about violence, spiritual defilement, and corruption, all without lingering on the topic of Thomas Kintry's brutal murder. Though *The Exorcist III* at first tries to make some muddled statement about the violent racist scourge at the center of American history, it forgets this point about thirty minutes in and instead returns once again to the grand metaphysical battle between Man and Evil.

•

In this way, *The Exorcist* is an evasion. The film presents evil as something fundamentally intangible and mystical, a numinous threat to humanity rather than something humanity does to itself, made and remade every day in countless small but vast and infinitely interconnected ways. *The Exorcist* is America refusing to look at itself in the mirror and instead deflecting a vague spiritual notion of evil onto the body a rich white girl. It is a distraction, a manipulation, a lie.

Baldwin writes, "Americans should certainly know more about evil than that; if they pretend otherwise, they are lying, and any black man, and not only blacks—many, many others, including white children—can call them on this lie; he who has been treated as the devil recognizes the devil when they meet." This is what *The Exorcist* trilogy misses: Evil is not something amorphous or incorporeal. Evil is active. It is a doing, and then a doing again and again and again.

Just look, Baldwin says, at a cotton field, or a prison, or Vietnam. Just look at yourself.

•

Seen in another way, however, rather than a mere deflection, *The Exorcist* is also the loudest and most terrifying reflection of post-1960s white American resentment and rage. If, as Carol Anderson argues in *White Rage: The Unspoken Truth of Our Racial Divide,* America's history is marked by the violent

push-and-pull between Black political advancement and brutal white backlash, then Regan can also be understood as the
snarling and vengeful embodiment of white anger at the gains
made by Black Americans in the decades following the civil
rights movement. Looking at the possessed Regan now, I sometimes think of the infamous photograph of the white fifteen-
year-old Hazel Massery screaming at Elizabeth Eckford as she
enters the newly integrated Little Rock High School in 1957,
her face grotesquely contorted with viciousness and hate.

When Americans saw the bitter, ugly, and furious Regan
MacNeil growling at the world that Christmas, they saw a version of themselves, but rather than looking closely, they ran
away.

•

"It is time for an honest look at the problem of order in the
United States," says Richard Nixon in a now famous campaign ad from 1968 called the First Civil Right.

As he speaks, dark images flash across the screen: red police
lights, burning buildings, smoke-filled air. Blood runs down the
faces of screaming white men. The upper half of a female man-
nequin lies naked in a garbage strewn street. Shrill, dissonant
piano notes trill beneath the voiceover, punctuated by staccato
drumbeats that eventually build into a blaring, spine-tingling
roar. The ad skillfully employs the tools of horror to instill in
its viewers a sense of danger and unease, to create the fear that
something dangerous is waiting in the shadows. Watching it,
your chest tightens, even if you are someone who considers
yourself immune to such political mind tricks. This is what an
ad like this is designed to do: to make you fear for your life.

"Let us recognize that the First Civil Right of every American is to be free from domestic violence," the voice-over says.
"So I pledge to you: We *shall* have order in the United States."

The ad then advises viewers to "vote like your whole world depended upon it."

The First Civil Right represents perhaps the finest and most striking distillation of Nixon's Southern strategy: mobilize white anxiety and rage for your own political gains. Barry Goldwater and George Wallace had done it before Nixon, and Ronald Reagan would do it not long after. After Wallace attempted to block the enrollment of Black students at the University of Alabama, he received an outpouring of support from across the country. This sparked a eureka moment in which Wallace is said to have exclaimed, "They all hate Black people. All of them. They are afraid, all of them. Great God! That's it! They're all Southern! The whole United States is Southern!"

When Nixon saw the ad, he reportedly told his staff that it "hits it right on the nose. . . . It's all about law and order and the damn Negro and Puerto Rican groups out there." Though not a single person of color appears in Nixon's ad, the message is clear. As Anderson writes, "Crime and blackness soon became synonymous in carefully constructed ways that played to the barely subliminal fears of darkened, frightening images flashing across the screen." It was a deeply racist strategy cleansed of any overt racism, instead relying on coded language and symbols about schools, crime, urban unrest, and welfare to instill in white Americans the fear that *their* way of life, *their* civil rights, were in peril. Such rhetoric and imagery stoked white anxiety and justified the brutal and punitive carceral backlash that followed.

To be politically palatable after the liberal and socially conscious 1960s, white rage was now articulated as fear. But fear is just as dangerous as hate, and oftentimes it is the exact same thing. Though the narrative of imperiled white America was a carefully constructed fiction, people believed it. As a child,

I believed it: I spent many nights frozen in fear that, at any moment, my safe and beautiful suburban home could be beset by some unimaginably horrific invasion.

From the 1970s onward, white America recast itself as the helpless, endangered victim, a delusion reflected in horror movie after horror movie in which a terrified white person is running for their life, or in which a hearty white suburban family finds themselves under siege by mutants or psychopaths or ghosts. By perpetuating the lie that middle-class white families, arguably the safest and most secure sector of American society, were in fact no longer safe and secure, horror worked on a subconscious level to invigorate the calls for law and order that were echoing throughout the political sphere and causing unprecedented levels of devastation in communities of color. With hate reenvisioned as fear, large swaths of America no longer had to question the societal order or the nascent rage simmering in their own hearts. They only had to scream.

•

At the end of *The Exorcist*, a few days after the terrifying ordeal has finally come to a close, Chris and Regan pack their things into a car and prepare to leave the house on 3600 Prospect Street. As they do so, Father Dyer arrives to say goodbye. Regan thanks him and sweetly kisses his hand. It is a moment of hope: Chris will go on making successful films, Regan will go on reaping the social and financial benefits. The white girl is saved, and we are meant to feel relief.

The film is sure to remind viewers, the ones who made it to the end, that Regan has no memory of her possession, and so she will never have to reckon with its grisliness, its violence, its horror.

The girl has seen real evil, has been real evil, and yet she remembers nothing.

•

Baldwin himself was not a fan of the many Blaxploitation horror films that emerged on screens during the 1970s. In *The Devil Finds Work*, he writes, "I suspect their intention to be lethal indeed." However, if he were alive in 2017, I wonder if Baldwin would have been a fan of *Get Out*, a film that in many ways upholds the tradition of Black horror that preceded it. In *Get Out*, a family of white sociopaths brag about voting for Obama but then use the bodies of Black men and women to gain strength and immortality. Peele brilliantly flips the script on the predominant narratives of the genre, locating his horror not in a monster or a demon or a serial killer but in whiteness itself. *Get Out* gives many of the arguments Baldwin puts forth in *The Devil Finds Work* radical and thrilling form.

If evil exists in America, Baldwin argues, it is not in the "mindless and hysterical banality" displayed in *The Exorcist*. The real horror, Baldwin says, is in whiteness unexamined, in whiteness unquestioned, in whiteness coddled and protected and cordoned off from the long history of its own cruelty. In whiteness allowed to look away and forget.

Part 3

✠

PROFESSION OF FAITH

THE PRIESTS OF MY YOUTH

I was baptized by Father Cieslinski at Saint Patrick's Catholic Church in Canby, Oregon, my mother's hometown. She wore khaki slacks and a hot-pink polo shirt to the ceremony, her thick auburn hair blown out to a voluminous sheen. In one photo from that day, Father Cieslinski pours an oily trickle of holy water onto my forehead while my mother looks on, beaming. Father Cieslinski is sagging and liver spotted, elaborately frocked in flowing robes of beige, gold, and burgundy. In another photo, my mother gazes down at my swaddled red body, worrying the holy water into my skin with her matching hot-pink-nail-polished thumb. Father Cieslinski hovers behind her and seems to nod, as if to say, *Yes. Very Good. Keep Going.*

I wonder how long they stood there like that, gently rubbing. Maybe they believed that the deeper the holy water seeped, the longer its powers would last, filling up my pores and forming a protective seal to block out whatever sin would eventually and inevitably creep its way in.

•

The Exorcist is not called *The Possessed*. It would be an entirely different film if it were. Though twelve-year-old Regan

MacNeil provides the film's most potent and terrifying images, *The Exorcist* is about everyone *around* her, everyone *but* her: her atheist, movie-star mother Chris MacNeil; the movie-loving detective William Kinderman, who is investigating the death of director Burke Dennings; and most obviously, the two priests: Father Lankester Merrin, the more experienced exorcist, and Father Damien Karras, a younger priest in the midst of an intense crisis of faith. Regan MacNeil is little more than a body in a bed, a convenient plot device used to bring all the other characters, primarily the beleaguered Father Karras, further along on their spiritual journey.

The plot of *The Exorcist* trades off between shocking depictions of Regan's bloody descent into demonic possession and Father Karras's more stoic and pained descent into religious doubt, guilt, and grief. These two plots deftly intertwine, one responding to the next like a conversation, until they ultimately converge and implode.

While the spectacle of female possession is all surfaces—all body and its various putrid secretions—the story of male spiritual crisis is a logical progression that delves deep into Father Karras's spiraling mind and soul. Look at it one way and the demonic possession is nothing more than a spectacular backdrop to Damien Karras's intense emotional turmoil: his guilt over the death of his mother, his wavering devotion to the Catholic Church, his feelings of purposelessness and passivity, and something else, some other kind of darkness lurking within him that we sense but never fully understand. But the more I watch the film, the more I see something roiling and untethered in Karras too, a psyche as convulsive and pained on the inside as anything that happens to Regan's helpless body on the outside.

The two plots need each other. One cannot exist without the other.

•

In kindergarten, I began attending Sacred Trinity, a Catholic grade school and parish located in a quiet, middle-class Portland suburb. The school was small and dingy, with dark stairwells, stained brown carpets, and buzzing fluorescent lights. For years, the cafeteria doubled as the gymnasium. Eventually, though, the Parish raised enough money to construct an entirely new church building, complete with brilliant stainedglass windows, a large baptismal font, and excruciatingly detailed oil paintings of the Stations of the Cross. After that, the old church became the gym, and the cafeteria stayed the cafeteria.

Still, something haunted and shadowy lingered about the place. In the minds of Sacred Trinity's female students, Bloody Mary was not the vengeful ghost of England's Mary I but the mutilated apparition of the Holy Virgin herself. If there was any school bathroom in the universe where her bloody green visage would appear in the scratched mirrors after being called forth three times, it was Sacred Trinity.

Here, within the dimly lit halls of that squat brick building, we learned the majesty and grace of Christ. We were taught about God creating the earth in seven days and Jesus healing men of their leprosy the same way we were taught about the shifting of tectonic plates or the four ventricles of the heart: as natural and indisputable fact. Jesus was as real to me as George Washington or Thomas Edison were, only with cooler powers. I enjoyed religion class because it was basically story time mixed with arts and crafts. I saw Jesus less as a supernatural being to worship and praise and more as a series of blank outlines on a worksheet to color in with crayon.

Even as a young child, I was aware that there was no place for my mother or me in the Sacred Trinity after which my school was named. Perhaps for this reason, I gravitated more toward the brilliant suffering of the female martyrs—Saint Agnes, burned at the stake, Saint Blandina, gored to death by a raging steer, Saint Lucy, eyes gouged out and artfully displayed on a platter—and toward the quiet dignity of the Holy Virgin herself. I owned a book called *The Visions of Our Lady* that was full of oil paintings depicting the various Marion apparitions: Our Lady of Guadalupe, Our Lady of Mount Carmel, Our Lady of Fatima, Our Lady of the Golden Heart. I loved flipping through it and marveling at Mary's fabulous outfits. Sometimes, Mary appeared wearing flowing gold robes. Sometimes, she wore a gorgeous navy gown dotted with white stars. Sometimes, snow fell around her as she levitated on a cloud.

The school had one priest, Father Wheelan, a gentle, towering old man with a faint Irish accent who chain-smoked cigarettes by the playground. It also had one nun, Sister Marie Bernadette, an ancient woman whose brittle exterior betrayed the sheer force of her signature move, "the pincher," which involved grabbing misbehaving students by the meat of their upper arms with two fingers and then dragging them off to a quiet, dark place where they could wait out their punishment in silence. I fell victim to the pincher only twice in nine years: once, while I was giggling with my friend Heather Hamilton during Mass, and another, when I courageously scaled across the top of the monkey bars instead of swinging from them as designed.

"You'll break your arm," Sister Bernadette said, squeezing my bicep so hard I thought I might pass out.

Compared to the sanctimonious corporeal might of our resident nun, Father Wheelan was a warm and undemanding presence at the school, though one that commanded absolute respect. He lived in a cream-colored portable home in the back corner of the school parking lot. Whenever students were assigned to bring him something during the day—I can't for the life of me recall what we were bringing him—it was considered the utmost honor. I remember the portable home smelled like smoke and sweet hard candies, which I'd roll about in my mouth for the rest of the day, desperate to make them last as long as possible.

My mother and Father Wheelan were close. She would often slip into the sacristy before Sunday Mass to chat with him as he slid into his richly colored robes. Father Wheelan had been a source of support after her first cancer diagnosis, counseling her throughout her chemotherapy and recovery. Every Christmas, she brought him a bottle of fine County Mayo whiskey to remind him of home. My mother's casual and affectionate relationship with the school priest made me feel special, as if our family had been singled out as especially deserving of divine grace.

And yet I was far from a devout child. I hated going to Sunday Mass only slightly less than I hated sitting down to practice piano. The church always reeked of body odor and breast milk, and I dreaded the moment when I would have to shake hands with a stranger and extend an offering of peace. My own father was a committed nonbeliever, and so my brother Charley and I could often convince our mother to let the three of us stay home and make pancakes while she attended Sunday Mass alone. She'd return a few hours later, smelling of candlewax and ash. I think Father Wheelan was charmed by the solitary nature of her devotion. I got the sense that she told him things she didn't tell anyone else.

Perhaps for this reason, I often noticed an unspoken criticism radiating off Father Wheelan toward me, the soulless child who made her mother go to Mass alone. At monthly Confession, I felt condemned before I'd even said a word. Each time, I braced against the hot rot of his breath and asked for forgiveness. I concocted the usual lines about not practicing piano and being mean to my little brother. Though it was true that I seldom practiced piano and that Charley and I argued often, these confessions didn't quite articulate the sense of wrong-doing I felt boiling deeper inside me. It was a primordial guilt, blacker and thicker and harder to define. Something that even then I sensed had everything to do with my mother.

•

The first time we see Father Karras, he is standing on the Georgetown campus, watching Chris MacNeil shoot a scene for the student protest film *Crash Course*. Karras smiles and laughs from the sidelines, amused by the chaos and theatrics of movie production. He is an intriguing if not obviously hand-some man, short and broad shouldered with hollow cheekbones and dark hair that falls into shadowy eyes. He looks vaguely European, like he could be a fisherman tossing nets into the Mediterranean.

As he turns to leave, we hear the sound of Chris's voice booming out her lines in the background.

"If you want to affect any change," her character hollers into a blow horn, "you have to do it *within* the system!"

Later that day, when Chris is walking back from work, she stops suddenly in front of a church gate, as if compelled. Father Karras is standing there in the leafy courtyard wearing a black cassock and talking to another downtrodden priest.

"There's not a day in my life where I don't feel like a total fraud," Father Karras tells him.

These words, it seems, are meant to comfort the other priest, but they are also our first indication that Karras is not perfectly content within the system he has yoked himself to. He is a man at odds with his vocation and with himself.

Before we can hear the rest of their conversation, a train blares by somewhere in the distance. Chris hurries away.

We later learn that Father Karras is both a priest and a psychiatric therapist at the Georgetown seminary, providing counseling services to other men preparing to enter the priesthood. Karras lives in a cramped and dimly lit dorm room on campus, sleeping in a tiny twin bed just like he did when he studied at Harvard. He drinks: in crowded student bars or from the bottles of scotch that his friend, Father Dyer, has snatched from the university president's office, the sin of theft instantly absolved. Some days, like the one after his mother's death, Karras gets so drunk that Father Dyer has to help him to bed.

A former boxer, Karras stays fit by jogging at the school track in the mornings, clad in thick gray sweats like something out of *Rocky*. Watching Karras, we get the sense that he has not entirely forfeited the flesh in the way that his profession demands. As played by Jason Miller, a former milkman turned Pulitzer Prize–winning playwright, there is something rugged and animal about Karras's on-screen presence. Though Friedkin initially thought Miller was too short for the role, his compact frame lends a buzzing intensity to what otherwise could have been a dull and sexless character. He is like a piston, or a wolverine bucking against its too small cage.

Father Karras's first name, Damien, has created confusion for some viewers. Damien also happens to be the name of the possessed little boy in *The Omen*, released in 1976, three years after *The Exorcist*. As a result, many have mistakenly associated Damien Karras with the Anti-Christ and suggested that the "death mask" image that flashes subliminally across the screen throughout the film is in fact actor Jason Miller done up in full demon makeup.

This, however, is a misreading. The name Damien actually derives from the Greek word *damianos,* from which we get the word *daman*: to subdue, or tame.

•

To my First Communion, I wore a puffy-sleeved white dress with faux-pearl embroidery, white patent leather Mary Janes, and a jasmine flower crown my mother special ordered from the florist and had to store in the fridge. In a photo she snapped right before we left for the church, I'm holding a felt banner I'd made at Sunday School that says *God is Love.* My front teeth have mostly grown in, but one is longer than the other and they are separated by an almost goofily large gap. I felt beautiful and woozy and light-filled on that day.

At the ceremony, tears streamed down my eyes as I proceeded down the aisle to receive the Eucharist from Father Wheelan. Parents pointed and cooed from the pews.

"How adorable," they gasped. "She's *crying.*"

I don't recall knowing where the tears were coming from, but I remember the virtue I felt as they slid slowly down my cheeks. I looked over at my mother and saw that she was crying too, her gray-blue eyes glassy as she held up the camera and snapped another photo.

When I reached the front of the procession, Father Wheelan kneeled down and held out the small Communion wafer. Seeing my tears, his face lit up in a way I felt certain was reserved only for me.

"The Body of Christ," he said. His voice was as sonorous as a consecration.

"Amen," I responded, the words catching in my throat. I took the wafer and let the dry cardboard circle melt to nothing on my tongue.

Afterward, the second graders crowded together on the

church lawn for a group photo. I felt dizzy and began sneezing uncontrollably. My eyes swelled nearly shut, the wall of camera-wielding parents before me fading to a watery blur.

It was then determined that I had not been crying out of prismatic love for Christ but because I was having a severe allergic reaction to the special-ordered jasmine flower crown I was wearing on my head. My mother grabbed me from the lawn, tossed the crown into the trash, and led me to the bathroom in the church foyer, where she flushed out my eyes and gave me a Claritin. She was oddly gruff, angry almost, like she was disappointed that my tears had misled not only her but the entire congregation, that they had been a lie.

She'd left the bathroom door open, and when I raised my dripping face up from the sink, I saw, reflected in the mirror, Father Wheelan watching us from just beyond the doorway. My mother pulled paper towels from the dispenser and blotted them across my face. By the time we stepped back into the foyer, Father Wheelan was gone.

•

Priest films tend to fall into four basic categories: stories about an exorcism, stories depicting a crisis of faith within the priest and the religious community, stories of crime and/or murder, and stories involving an intimate, intense, and sometimes romantic relationship between a priest and one of his female parishioners. *The Exorcist* is unique in that it contains elements of all four. There is, of course, the possession and eventual exorcism of Regan MacNeil. There is Father Karras's own crisis of faith as well as the hinted-at crisis of faith within the seminarians at Georgetown. There's the murder of film director Burke Dennings, which is likely committed by the possessed Regan. And finally, there is the relationship between Father Karras and Chris MacNeil, which, though never explicitly romantic, is marked by a palpable and scintillating physical tension.

Priests have made regular appearances on screen throughout cinema history. Early depictions of priests in American film tend to be sunny and church-approved, such as those in the uncomfortably colonial *The Kingdom* or the good-hearted musical dramas *Going My Way* and *The Bells of St. Mary's,* two films Pauline Kael referenced in her scathing review of *The Exorcist* as recruiting posters for the Catholic Church. By midcentury, priest roles in film darkened slightly. With *On the Waterfront* and Hitchcock's *I Confess,* we see early examples of the murder and/or crime plotline, which endures in later films like *True Confessions* and *Primal Fear.*

The Europeans tend to be more staid in their depictions of priests: fewer musical numbers, more dour silences. In Robert Bresson's *Diary of a Country Priest,* an ascetic and sickly young priest who consumes nothing but bread and wine is diagnosed with stomach cancer and eventually dies in the home of a lapsed priest living in sin with a beautiful woman. In Ingmar Bergman's *Winter Light,* which stars *The Exorcist*'s Max von Sydow, a priest struggles with his looming feelings of doubt while fending off the overwhelming affections of a parishioner named Marta. By far the raciest of these is *Léon Morin, Priest,* about the chaste but all-consuming relationship that forms between a priest and a woman in Nazi-occupied France. Jean-Paul Belmondo, while not a particularly convincing priest, lends a labial carnality to the film that ups its erotic factor by several notches.

We now see these types of intense priest-woman relationships play out mainly on TV shows like *The Sopranos* or *Fleabag.* In these stories, a woman turns to a priest for the type of emotional support she is not receiving elsewhere. She finds comfort and freedom in a relationship with a man that is not based solely around courtship or sex. The priests, in turn, grow to need these relationships, to define themselves as "good priests" in relation to them. It is a way to be close to a woman without breaking the vow of celibacy. There is also a hint of manipulation at play: The priests form deep bonds with women, all the while knowing that their ultimate devotion is to the Lord. The powerful absence of sex in an otherwise cloyingly intense emotional bond tends to spark confusion for both parties, mainly for the women. Carmela Soprano dumps the baked ziti she'd cooked for Father Intintola into the trash after she sees him speaking intimately with another woman in the confessional. She had thought their wine-and-movie nights had been special, something for just the two of them.

Most priest-woman stories are tales of frenzied female confession and desire met with stoic male reserve and denial. The typical roles are reversed: The woman pursues, the man demurs. In *Sex and the City,* Samantha feverishly stalks Friar Fuck until he informs her that his body, while perfect in all its splendor, is made for other joys. *Fleabag* is radical in that Fleabag and Hot Priest actually break his vow of celibacy and have sex, but the relationship is nonetheless doomed when Hot Priest declares that he loves God more than he loves her. Very few, if any, priest stories show the man leaving the priesthood and rejoining the secular world.

Thanks to the lasting popularity of *The Exorcist,* priests have also become a mainstay in the horror genre, playing necessary roles in everything from *The Amityville Horror* to *The Exorcism of Emily Rose.* The horror genre remained the prominent source of priestly cinematic representation up until the early twenty-first century, when priests began to be associated with a different kind of horror unfolding on screen. Films like *Doubt* and *Spotlight* mirror the shift in our cultural understanding of priests away from the good and upright bearers of

light to something darker and more morally ambiguous, sometimes even evil.

•

Father Wheelan left the parish when I was in the sixth grade.
He was replaced by Father Ben, who had a nasally voice,
white-blonde hair, and a protruding stomach that he liked to
rub when he talked.

On the first all-school mass of the year, which was often
attended by parents and other parishioners in addition to the
student body, Father Ben stood before us on the altar and
announced that everything we had ever learned about the Sign
of the Cross was wrong. The Holy Spirit does not reside in our
chests, he explained, but rather deep, deep inside our bellies,
even beyond them. He stepped to the right of the altar ledge
and demonstrated proper form: one light touch to forehead and
both shoulder blades before lowering his hands far down past
his hip bones to what my mother called "the crotchal region."
He then led students through the proper steps, refusing to continue the Mass until we followed along. We exchanged confused glances, waiting for the parents or teachers to intervene.

"In the name of the Father, the Son, and—"

Father Ben stopped, watching us and gesturing with his
hands.

"Lower," he instructed in a deep baritone. "Lower . . .
lower."

A wave of uniformed grade schoolers tentatively reached
their hands down to their pleated navy trousers.

"The Holy Spirit," Father Ben signed, satisfied.

This set Father Ben off on the wrong foot with the student body, who remained suspicious of him from there on out.
Unlike Father Wheelan, who wore the traditional clerical collar and black slacks when not delivering mass, Father Ben wore

Italian loafers and candy-colored silk shirts that he tucked into jeans and a braided belt. Every few months, he would drop into our sixth-grade classroom unannounced to deliver the same rambling monologue about puberty and premarital sex. Father Ben would opine about all the ways our bodies were changing—growing hair and fat in new places, starting to smell in ways they'd never smelled before—and explain that this meant we were emerging from the innocent light of childhood and into the tumultuous darkness of adolescence.

One day, while delivering such a speech, Father Ben slowly began unbuckling his braided belt while standing directly in front of Christopher Deluca, widely acknowledged to be the handsomest kid in our sixth-grade class.

"You are probably starting to have sexual feelings," he said, sliding the belt strap slowly out of the buckle. "You may find yourself wanting to do bad things with other little boys and girls."

He pulled up his khakis and readjusted them slightly before continuing.

"You must never act on these feelings," he said. "See them as God's challenge. A chance to rise above our sinful natures and live in the purity and grace of Christ."

Father Ben then began slowly rebuckling his belt, all the while telling us not to touch ourselves or indulge in unholy thoughts. Christopher sat frozen in his desk. Everyone in the class watched, aghast. Our teacher, Miss Russell, said nothing.

The truth was that I was having unholy thoughts that spring, about Christopher Deluca of all people. When Father Ben spoke to the class about unholy thoughts, I felt that he was calling me out personally, that somehow he knew the strange and surprising dreams I'd started having about Christopher Deluca's bare stomach.

Each year during Lent, the current sixth-grade class held

a public performance in which they reenacted the Stations of the Cross for the parish. It was the biggest event of the year, complete with costumes and set pieces and musical accompaniment, by which I mean a boombox in the corner that played an instrumental CD someone had bought at a Christian bookstore ten years before. The boys would become Roman soldiers, donning helmets crested with red fans and strappy sandals that tied around the calves. The girls dressed up in teal- and rose-colored robes and tied scarves around their heads with strands of rope. There were no speaking roles in the Stations of the Cross. Instead, during each Station—Jesus Is Condemned to Death, or Jesus Falls for the Third Time, or Jesus Meets His Sorrowful Mother—a student would step up to a microphone on the altar and read a short prayer. While they did so, the corresponding sixth graders would gather on the stage and assume the proper pose—Pontius Pilot pointing an accusatory finger at Jesus, Jesus stumbling with the cross over his back, Mary kneeling before her son in tears—while another kid scurried to the boombox and pressed play. The students would then hold the pose for sixty seconds or so, during which the congregation was to silently reflect on the suffering Jesus endured.

The role of Jesus always went to the skinniest, whitest, and best-looking kid in the class. Our year, the role went to Christopher Deluca. Christopher and the rest of our class were under a lot of pressure to perform, as our year coincided with the release of Mel Gibson's *The Passion of the Christ*, in which Jesus's suffering was displayed with graphic glee: torture porn for uber-devoted Catholics. My mom wouldn't let me see the film, but my friend Heather Hamilton had seen it, and I remember feeling nauseated when she told me that the film actually showed the nails going *in*. Hard to compete with that.

When Miss Russell announced the cast, I was chagrined to learn that I had been cast as one of the Sanhedrin, a boring and thankless role that was supposed to go to a boy. I had always fashioned myself a Mary or a Veronica. Still, being a member of the Sanhedrin had its perks. Since my part only required me to appear in two Stations, I could spend most of rehearsals standing on the sidelines and watching.

My favorite Station was always Jesus Is Stripped of His Garments, because the boy Roman soldiers would actually strip the boy Jesus on stage. There was something titillating about seeing Christopher, a boy whom I only ever saw dressed in navy pants and a starchy white polo, totally disrobed, his soft, child's tummy bared for all to see. I liked how vulnerable he looked up there, how cold.

The afternoon following Father Ben's visit to our class, I told my mother about how he'd removed his belt in front of Christopher.

"You're exaggerating," she said.

I was taken aback that she wasn't instantly on my side. I'd noticed that she didn't visit Father Ben before Mass like she'd done with Father Wheelan, and many parents in the parish seemed just as wary of him as the students. This was only a few years after the *Globe* story put sexual abuse within the church at the forefront of the national conversation, and though most students did not understand the details of the decades-long cover-up, we had nonetheless grown suspicious of priests, especially priests like Father Ben. No one wanted to make deliveries to the portable home in the parking lot anymore.

When I insisted that I wasn't exaggerating, that Father Ben really had unbuckled his belt in front of Christopher, the boy Jesus, she took a deep breath and sighed.

"You shouldn't talk that way about our priest," she said.

Within the year, Father Ben was transferred to another parish and replaced by Father Dan, a decently handsome, prematurely gray priest whom my mother once again started visiting in the sacristy. It was never entirely clear why Father Ben left. The student body was just grateful that he was gone. As far as we knew, Father Ben hadn't done anything to anyone, but with his high-pitched voice and colorful silk T-shirts, he had made us uncomfortable, and that was enough.

Years later, my brother Charley and I stayed up late on our porch one night, drinking beer and discussing memories from our Sacred Trinity days. Several few drinks in, we tipsily stumbled upon the long-forgotten topic of Father Ben. We began crudely speculating about whom, if anyone, he would have molested at Sacred Trinity. After about our fifth beer, we narrowed it down to either Christopher or Andrew O'Brien, whose dad had renovated our kitchen.

We briefly toyed with the idea of starting a podcast called Finding Father Ben, in which we would interrogate our blurry memories of him and interview people from within the local Catholic community. Was Father Ben really dangerous, we'd ask, or had the conservative parish ousted an innocent man because they found him strange? Had Father Ben hurt anyone, or was it the priesthood itself causing irreparable harm? We envisioned lots of children's chamber choirs as the interstitial music and a black-and-white banner image of a priest clutching a rosary near his crotchal region.

To jumpstart our research, we drunkenly went down the rabbit hole of searching for Father Ben's whereabouts online. After a quick search, we discovered that Father Ben had worked at several parishes after leaving Sacred Trinity before eventually settling as a chaplain at a nursing home. In a grainy photo from the nursing home bulletin, a white-haired Father Ben leans over an old woman in a hospital bed, gently resting his hand on her shoulder and smiling.

•

In a busy bar, Father Karras, still dressed in his clerical collar, grabs two foamy pints and sits down at a booth with another priest, Father Tom. The bar is mostly filled with Georgetown students. "Ramblin' Man" by the Allman Brothers plays faintly in the background.

Karras needs that drink. He has just come from visiting his mother in her crumbling tenement apartment in Manhattan. She is recovering from a serious foot injury, and she spends her days laying prone in an armchair, listening to the radio alone. On her walls hang photos of a shirtless young Damien in his boxing gear, looking determined and fierce. Father Karras stares at these old photos of himself with longing.

At the bar, he first tells Father Tom that he wants a reassignment, possibly to somewhere in New York so he can be closer to his mother. Soon after, he admits that he may want out of the job altogether.

It is a startling confession for a priest to make. You can see the weight of it twisting across Father Karras's face. His inability to successfully counsel the aspiring priests at the seminary is wrapped up with his inability to properly care for his ailing mother, which is wrapped up with his inability to find meaning and satisfaction in his own life, which is inexplicably wrapped up with Chris MacNeil, the short-haired actress who has just arrived in the neighborhood and who watches him from the streets.

"It's more than psychiatry, Tom," Father Karras continues. "Some of their problems come down to faith. Their vocation. The meaning of their lives."

It isn't entirely clear if Karras is talking about his students or himself. This, however, gets at the very heart of his crisis.

Something is wrong with the Catholic priesthood, with what it does to the men who enter it. Through the struggling seminarians at Georgetown, Karras begins not only to doubt his own faith but the priesthood as a whole. There is something prophetic and raw about *The Exorcist*'s casual acknowledgement that the priesthood is difficult and perhaps even wrong, that the vocation is lonely and unsustainable for even the most devoted, that maybe the system itself is deeply broken. After counseling so many tortured future priests, Karras is beginning to suspect that there is something warped about the institution and its demands. Maybe the seminarians should be out drinking in rowdy bars, flirting and listening to the Allman Brothers instead of studying ancient biblical texts in dark dorms, readying themselves for lives of poverty and celibacy. Maybe the young seminarians, and as a result, some past version of Father Karras, are among the church's flailing victims.

"I can't cut it anymore," Karras tells Father Tom. "I need out. I'm unfit."

He then adds, almost as an afterthought, "I think I've lost my faith."

•

My mother was promiscuous with her priests. Though she regularly visited with Father Dan at Sacred Trinity, she remained close with Father Wheelan years after he'd left the Parish. When her father died, she asked Father Wheelan to preside over his burial. I was fifteen, and my grandpa was the first dying person I'd ever seen. When I visited him a few days before his death, his cheeks were sunken, and his skin was a shocking shade of yellow. His wife, my mother's stepmother, had brought his bed into the center of the living room, and I took a nervous seat by his side.

Though he couldn't speak, he smiled and reached out a

shaking hand. I took it, managing a meek smile, but I broke into a cold sweat, terrified. During a sleepover with my friend Nicole Smith a few days later, my sobs woke her up in the middle of the night.

"His skin was so yellow," I wailed.

On the foggy morning of his burial, my mom, brother, and I drove out to the small Canby cemetery. As we pulled up to the cemetery, Father Wheelan stood hunched among the gravestones, smoking a cigarette. When he saw us, he crushed his cigarette under his heel and walked toward our car.

"Mary," Father Wheelan said gently, reaching out his arms and folding my mother in a gentle embrace. He greeted Charley and turned to me. With my mother and brother watching, he leaned down and kissed me directly on the mouth. His lips were cracked and dry, the tender skin peeling off in little strips. I was too shocked to move. Out of the corner of my eye, I saw my mother flinch and then straighten. Though it was a chaste, closed-mouth kiss, a gust of smoke and whiskey peeled down my throat as he pulled away. Charley grimaced. My mother avoided eye contact as we followed Father Wheelan to the grave site.

As they lowered my grandpa's casket into the ground, I replayed the three-second kiss over and over again in my head. Maybe it was an accident, I told myself: He was going for my cheek and missed. Why else would he have done it with my mother two feet away, and why else would she have barely reacted at all? Or maybe this was routine, just something priests did to all women when they turned fifteen. My mother had recently informed me that I was "putting on weight," and I had yet to be asked to homecoming or on a date by any of the boys I feverishly journaled about at night, so clearly, I told myself, I was too freckled and rotund for Father Wheelan's kiss to be anything but a formal, sexless adult greeting.

I avoided looking directly at him as he read from his Bible during the ceremony. Occasionally, though, we locked eyes. When we did, my face burned hot with shame.

"Did you see Father Wheelan kiss me on the mouth?" I asked my mother on the drive home. I was sitting next to her in the front seat. "Why didn't you say anything?"

My mother paused. She fanned her fingers out over the wheel and then gripped it tightly, the skin over her knuckles growing taut and white.

"Just drop it," she finally said.

"So you *did* see it?" I replied, my voice indignant and high.

"You're being selfish," my mother snapped. She was still looking ahead at the road. "For once, this day isn't about you."

With that, I fell into a silent, sizzling rage.

I couldn't tell who I was angrier at: Father Wheelan or my mother.

•

In an early scene in the movie, an unnamed priest strides into a church with two giant bouquets of flowers in each arm. He genuflects in front of the altar before placing one bouquet on its farthest right side. As he turns toward the Virgin Mary statue on the left, he lets out a horrified gasp.

Two orange traffic cones protrude from the Virgin's body where her breasts should be. A beaked spear wrenches itself from her crotch like a phallus. Thick black paint trickles down from it, poisoned blood. Her outstretched hands drip red.

Frightened, the priest stumbles and backs away toward the exit.

Later, Detective William Kinderman meets Father Karras at the school track, where Karras has just gone for a run. Kinderman suspects that the desecration at the church and the probable murder of director Burke Dennings are somehow connected. Dennings was found at the bottom of the staircase outside the house on 3600 Prospect Street with his head turned completely around on his neck. Kinderman knows that Father Karras once wrote a psychiatric paper on witchcraft and might offer some insight on the matter. What Kinderman really wants to know: Is the desecration the work of witches participating in a Black Mass or of a deranged priest unconsciously rebelling against the church?

Father Karras shakes his head. Even if he knew a priest like that, which he insists he does not, he couldn't tell Kinderman anyway. It's a matter of confession, he explains. He made a vow.

At this point in the film, we've heard enough from Karras to know that what he's saying isn't exactly true. Many seminarians are in trouble. Their suffering surpasses his abilities both as a priest and as a psychiatrist. These men, they could do anything.

Still, he will do what he can to protect them.

•

During my junior year in high school, I developed a reputation for my erotic fiction, which I would write and then circulate among my friends for their comic titillation. I had recently finished a masterpiece titled "Sex Island" about a plane that crashes onto a mystical island and the various romantic entanglements that ensue among the stranded passengers. It was basically *Lost,* but smuttier. The story began with a man and woman loudly fucking in the bathroom as the plane nosedived toward the Pacific, their cries of pleasure bleeding into terrified screams.

Once I finished "Sex Island," I embarked upon my most audacious piece yet: a novella entitled "O'Flanagahan's Folly." The story followed a recovering alcoholic named Regina as she joins a local parish and develops a sexual relationship with a handsome young priest, Father O'Flanagahan. In my rendering, Father O'Flanagahan's mouth was full and sweet, nothing like the dirty barroom floor that was Father Wheelan's. When Regina tempted him, he quivered under her fierce sexual power. She liked to sneak into the sacristy and guzzle wine from the church's box of Franzia before slyly coaxing Father O'Flanagahan out of his silky robes. She liked to drizzle hot candle wax down Father O'Flanagahan's soft and agile back.

Though I had recently been confirmed and had taken on Bernadette as my saint's name, my devotion to the Catholic Church was at its nadir. I can't say exactly when or why I stopped believing, or even that I did so definitively. There was no great and shattering break, just a gradual and undramatic erosion of faith that culminated somewhat flamboyantly in the sacrilegious drafting of "O'Flanagahan's Folly." I found myself more drawn to the other spiritual traditions we'd learned about in our world religions class: Buddhism, with its constant reminder that life is suffering, or Hinduism, with its divine cycles of death and rebirth, or Judaism, with its unapologetic embrace of the Old Testament's blood, sex, and violence. By comparison, Catholicism seemed flimsy and hollow. In defiance, I would write a scene or two of "O'Flanagahan's Folly" over the weekend, print it out, and then bring it to class on Monday to show my friends, making sure none of the real priests who stalked the halls of our high school saw a thing.

After Sacred Trinity, I attended an expensive Jesuit high school located on a dull strip of highway lined with fast-food restaurants and adult entertainment businesses. It had its own crest and a pompous Latinate slogan: *Age Quod Agis,* or *Do well whatever you do,* which I took to heart when composing my erotic fiction.

"We're not better than other schools," the principal would

say at assemblies, standing before a wall of banners from the various sports championships we'd won over the years. "We're just different."

Sometimes kids from the nearby public high school would throw slices of bread or McDonalds bags at Jesuit students while they stood at the bus stop. Some Jesuit students took this as evidence that we upright Catholics were being unjustly persecuted by the bands of cruel heathens who pelted us with foodstuffs while they drove past in their used cars, but I understood their motivation. Alfred Hitchcock once said of his own Jesuit education, "I spent three years studying with the Jesuits. They used to terrify me to death. Now I'm getting my own back by terrifying other people." The Jesuits were indeed an excruciating combination of strictness and self-regard, and I can relate to the enduring compulsion to stick it to them, even years after I've left their supposedly hallowed halls.

Though we were not required to wear uniforms, the dress code at Jesuit was tyrannical. If a girl ever broke it, say by showing her collarbone or wearing a skirt that did not reach at least two inches below the knee, she was forced to wear an absurdly baggy sweatshirt or oversized prairie skirt for the rest of the day. The offending female was met with snickers and suggestive winks wherever she walked, as if the new coverings emphasized rather than hid her transgression. Up until the mid-'90s, Jesuit had been an all-boys academy, and girls were still treated like an invasive species, constantly in danger of disturbing the sensitive native males.

Any type of rule violation, be it sartorial or otherwise, could earn one a JUG, which stood for Justice Under God. The punishment required the perpetrator to do things like wipe down the lunch tables with a dirty rag or stay after school to pick up trash around campus with one of those little pokers. I received only one JUG during my four years at Jesuit, when a sliver of my hot-pink bra strap was visible through the back of my white shirt. The teacher who administered the JUG wasn't entirely sure my violation qualified, and so he sent me to the principal, who stood up, examined me closely, and confirmed that I was indeed in violation. Receiving a JUG was always part shame, part pride. Yes, you had to endure the humiliation of public punishment, but your rebellion also earned you a certain amount of cachet among the student body. You bore it with dignity and good humor.

Once a year, each class went on a weekend retreat to Oregon's McKenzie River, where we would pray, sing around a bonfire, and if you were lucky, sneak off with the boy or girl of your choosing to make out on a mossy stump in the woods. The retreats were optional, but I went every year because I hoped that maybe *this* would be the year I finally got my midnight rendezvous. I never did, and so instead I endured the retreat's various bizarre rituals year after year, the most memorable of which involved lining up in a darkened hallway with our heads pressed up against the cold wall while plump, red-faced Father Allen asked us a long list of questions about our sins. We weren't supposed to answer aloud, merely to ponder our wrongdoing in stony silence. One year, however, my friend Sonja and I burst into raucous laughter when Father Allen asked, his voice stern as the cross in the pitch dark, "Have you ever touched yourself inappropriately?"

The weekly all-school masses were also optional. For my first two years at Jesuit, I went every Friday because, if you were strategic about it, you might get the chance to sit next to your crush and hold their hand during the Our Father. Mass also offered sixty free minutes to think about sex without the risk of a teacher calling on you to answer a question. You could just surrender to it. I reckon roughly 90 percent of the school was thinking about sex during Mass each Friday. You could taste it in the air, a goopy miasma hanging thick over our heads.

By junior year, I had realized that no matter how many times I squeezed hands with Aidan Foster or Blake Lewis during the Our Father, it would never translate into them asking me on a date. I gave up on going to Mass and instead spent the free period in the library with Sonja, doodling and composing "O'Flanagahan's Folly" when I was supposed to be doing my homework.

I took refuge in "O'Flanagahan's Folly." I found its narrative pull hilarious and all-consuming. It was my way of puncturing the oppressive Catholic piety that marked so much of my life, of artfully registering my own very conscious rebellion against patriarchal authority. I reveled in the absolute sacrilege of it: *a woman and a priest having sex*. Weird sex, too, often involving various sexual instruments that Regina left for O'Flanagahan in the tabernacle (I was careful, though, never to include any crucifixes among the props). There was something exciting to me about allowing the woman to possess riotous desire and positioning the man as the one who must hesitate and then give in, doing whatever the woman wanted and then feeling guilty or confused about it later. In "O'Flanagahan's Folly," it was Father O'Flanagahan's virginity that Regina took with sloppy, drunken enthusiasm. I think it was also a relief to turn sex into something comic and outrageous rather than something that would break both my hymen and my spirit, sending me down a long and corrupt path of abortion, self-destruction, and STDs. With "O'Flanagahan's Folly," I stumbled upon a silly and joyful kind of power, both as a narrator and as a young woman.

One afternoon, I walked into my bedroom and found my

mother standing by my desk with a small stack of paper in her hands. Her mouth was twisted tight, her brow furrowed in rage.

"What is this?" she asked.

I didn't need to look at the papers to know what she was reading: the second act of "O'Flanagahan's Folly," in which Regina hides beneath Father O'Flanagahan's cavernous robes during the Memorial Acclamation, bringing him to stuttering climax just as the congregation sings out, "Christ has died, Christ has risen, Christ will come again."

Can you get excommunicated for something like this? I wondered as I wrote it. Being excommunicated sounded kind of thrilling, like it should have been one of the sacraments.

"I can't believe something like this could come out of the mind of my own daughter," my mother said.

"It's a joke," I replied.

"Do you really think this is funny?" she said, shaking the papers as she took a step toward me.

"Kind of," I said with a shrug. "Isn't it?"

She stopped and looked down. Her eyes darted back and forth across the text. A faint shimmer of a smile flickered across he lips before she pulled them taut again.

"That's not the point," she said. "You could get expelled. I'm shredding it."

She strode out of the room with the pages in her hands. She must have known as well as I that the draft was saved to my computer.

•

About halfway through *The Exorcist,* Father Karras's elderly mother suffers an edema and is sequestered in the neuropsychiatric ward at New York's Bellevue Hospital. When Karras arrives for a visit, his uncle informs him that she has been screaming uncontrollably for hours and refusing to let the doctors touch her. He'd found her alone in her apartment, talking to her radio like it was a person.

"You know it's funny," the uncle says as they hurry down the fluorescent halls, passing distant-eyed patients in bathrobes who mumble to themselves and rock in their chairs, "If you weren't a priest, you'd be a famous psychiatrist now, Park Avenue, and your mother, she'd be living in a penthouse instead of here."

There it is again: another barbed reminder that Father Karras's noble profession isn't quite so noble after all. He may shepherd flocks of wayward souls for a living, but when it comes down to the people he loves most, he is failing.

Karras and his uncle watch the sick women in the ward through a barred window. It is an unsettling scene, one perfectly designed to play on societal fears of mental illness and the unwell female body. The room is full of women in white gowns, their hair frizzy and wild. One sits on her bed cross-legged, pointing at something invisible on the sheets. Another lies prone on the mattress, her head titled off to one side, looking just days away from death. Another rubs her tired eyes like you do when you've had a bad day, only it's clear that this woman has had nothing but bad days for a very, very long time. Even through the window Karras can hear their sobs and heaving. These women—women in acute crisis, women who are sick and vulnerable and alone—reflect Karras's own psychic turmoil. They are an exaggeration, an amplification, of his own perceived inability to help the one woman in his life who truly needs him.

When Karras enters the locked ward, the crying women come rushing toward him. They grab at him, raking their fingers down his black coat. Some reach out to him from their beds as if he is a saintly apparition: a man of the cloth, here to save them. Instead, Karras jerks his arm away and rushes toward his mother's bed in the back of the room. Goodness has its limits.

Something about this scene always reminds me of the moment in *The Shining* when Jack Torrance finally enters Room 237. In the scene, Jack follows the room's carpet, its bright purple and green pattern suspiciously phallic, to the bathroom. There he finds a beautiful, naked woman waiting for him in the bathtub. She slowly rises from the water and presses her firm, dripping body against his. Jack closes his eyes as they begin to kiss. When he opens them again, the beautiful woman has transformed into an old crone, her skin rotten and her gray hair falling from her head in chunks. Jack jumps away and dashes from the room, running upstream against the carpet dicks. She follows him with her distended stomach and flabby, outstretched arms, cackling like a witch.

Though this scene is obviously quite different from the one in *The Exorcist,* they reflect similar fears. The female body, usually displayed as a source of comfort or sexual desire, is instead transformed into something demanding and ugly, something ragged with want. It is a shock and a betrayal; the woman is no longer beautiful or soft like she should be, and yet she reaches her arms out to you anyway. These scenes make me think about how primed we are to see female suffering— female sadness and anger and longing and pain—as something monstrous, wrong, or maybe just inconvenient, and how easy this makes it for us to turn away.

When Karras finally finds his mother, she lies in a white gown on a bleached white bed. Her hair and eyebrows are white too. She looks like a child, helpless and small. Her arms have been bound to the bed, just as the possessed Regan's will be later in the film.

"Why you did this to me, Dimmy?" his mother asks when she sees him. "Why?"

The film cuts to a shot of Karras at the gym, hammering at a punching bag with his fists until he practically collapses. With every strike, Karras is thinking about his mother, and all the women, all those helpless, suffering women. How they'd needed his help, and how he had done nothing.

•

Father Frank claimed to possess the ability to speak in tongues. Though glossolalia is most often associated with the Pentecostal and Evangelical Christian faiths, some Catholics are known to do it too. Acceptance of the practice, like exorcism, seems cautious at best. It is mainly practiced among certain minority charismatic subsets who claim they've been unexpectedly blessed with the gift. Father Frank, however, was traditional and restrained, the last person you'd expect to break out into sudden divine babble. He was the oldest priest at Jesuit, and the most feared. He had a ruddy face and ring of gray hair. He looked at you with a disdain so strong and destabilizing that you would do whatever he asked just to prove you were worthy. Whenever I passed his stern face in the halls, he stared me down like I'd already failed at some task I wasn't even aware I'd been assigned.

Father Frank taught my section of Christian and Hebrew Scripture. Everyone always said that if you had Father Frank as your teacher for Christian and Hebrew Scripture, you might, once Pentecost rolled around, get to hear him speak in tongues. Father Frank would not unleash his gift just because somebody asked. He would only break it out at special moments, around people he believed deserved, or needed, to witness it. Most people spent four years at Jesuit without ever experiencing Father Frank's famed glossolalia. If you were in Father Frank's scripture class, however, your chances were believed to be far higher.

Lo and behold, the Friday before Pentecost, Father Frank strode into the classroom after the bell and announced he would be taking the first portion of class to show us his gift. We had just spent that week reading about the "mighty rushing wind" and the tongues of flame that appeared above the disciples' heads. Anticipation rippled across the room, and then the questions: What does it feel like? Does your mind just go blank? Can you really do it on command? Have you ever done it at the grocery store just to freak someone out?

"No," Father Frank responded. He moved a chair out from behind his desk and set it down in front of the blackboard. "I can only do it if I feel the person I lay hands upon is in need of a blessing. If I feel their life could benefit from the direct presence of the Holy Spirit."

His eyes scanned the classroom, up and down the rows. It did not for a second occur to me that I would be chosen. I was not usually picked out of crowds or singled out for any reason at all. I assumed he would choose someone more openly religious, or maybe someone more obviously troubled. When he said my name, I barely even heard it.

"Marly," he repeated, motioning to the chair. "Would you please join me?"

My stomach dropped. I looked helplessly across the room at Sonja, who widened her eyes in shock and then collapsed into stifled laughter. As I stood up from my chair and proceeded toward the front of the room, the class fell into an expectant and bemused silence. Some students smirked up at me in a *Sucks for you* kind of way. Others watched with genuine interest, perhaps even envy. I would have happily traded places with any of them. I resented being singled out as in special need of divine intervention. *Does he know about* "O'Flanagahan's Folly?" I wondered as I sat down.

"Good," Father Frank said, the warmth of his body pressing behind me. It felt wrong, that someone that cold and devout could emit human warmth. His hand lowered onto my head and gripped my skull. It was not the gentle laying on of hands I had expected. He grabbed my head like he was driving his fingers into the holes of a bowling ball. My body stiffened.

"Now I'd like you to close your eyes," he said, "and think of someone in your life who is in need of prayer."

That explains it, I thought. *My mother. He knows about my mother.*

It had only recently come to my explicit attention that my mother's cancer had returned. My parents hadn't told me about it directly, however. Instead, they informed my school counselor, Mr. Peters, a burly man fond of Lycra T-shirts and ill-fitting khakis, who doubled as the school's varsity football coach. Mr. Peters had then called me out of fifth-period physics and delivered the bad news himself, with the awkward warmth of a decent man thrown utterly out of his element.

I told Mr. Peters I had no idea that my mother's cancer was back. I said it like the disease was some horror movie villain who'd returned to the neighborhood or the summer camp after everyone thought they were safe. I said *her cancer* like it belonged to her.

Better Mr. Peters than us, my parents probably figured. Even in an era when the cultural awareness around breast cancer couldn't have been higher—when pink ribbons donned yogurt lids and buckets of chicken and oil rigs in the Gulf of Mexico, when even Pornhub claimed to donate a penny to a breast cancer charity for every thirty clicks on one of their "big breast" or "small breast" videos—the disease was still a taboo topic in my household. We did not speak of it. My parents avoided serious conversations like the plague, and cancer was about as serious as it could get. If they could outsource the work to the football coach, all the better.

"Sometimes parents don't tell you these things because they want to protect you," Mr. Peters scrambled, looking uncomfortable and overwhelmed.

I guessed this was true. It was also true that my mind had been elsewhere the past year or so. It wasn't like my mother was exactly *hiding* her illness. It's just that I was too busy getting high on the weekends and stealing lawn gnomes with my friends to care. If I'd been paying attention, I would have noticed the tired slump that had overtaken her posture and the hours she spent in her room "resting her eyes." I would have noticed how thin her hair looked pulled back in a scrunchie, and how her brain became so foggy that she forgot words like *butternut squash* and *wallet*. And I suppose I did notice these things, as I can pluck them clearly out of my memory now, but I didn't really absorb them, at least not as anything more than irrelevant background scenery to the larger drama of my adolescent life.

My mother and I fought often in those days, and accepting that she was sick, I mean really accepting it, would have meant making the effort to be a little less hostile and withdrawn. It would have meant treating her like someone deserving of compassion rather than someone who did my laundry. It would have meant not mocking her when she forgot the word for *butternut squash*. It would have meant forgiving her for telling me to lose weight and for refusing to speak to me for weeks after that one time I wasn't friendly enough to her friend Jennifer at the grocery store. At the very least, it would have meant thinking about her when Father Frank was Vulcan-gripping my skull.

But I didn't. I couldn't be bothered to think about my

mother in a time like this. All I could think about was the twenty-six eyes on me and the tight, kneading claw of Father Frank's fingers on my head. I felt a rush of adrenaline as he shifted behind me. He inhaled and exhaled, inhaled and exhaled. He was readying himself. My heart pounded in my chest. I winced proactively and lowered my eyes to my lap.

A galloping barrage of language burst forth from Father Frank's mouth. It sounded guttural and slobbery, with far more *b*'s and *f*'s than you might expect. His babble brought to mind a fish struggling to breath on dry land, or a plunger vigorously pumping a toilet bowl. It wasn't ecstatic. It was flatulent. It sounded like he was making it up as he went.

Emboldened by the absurdity of it, I looked up at the class. Some were wide-eyed with disbelief. Others cocked their heads in mild amusement. A few people scowled. The rest were so dead-eyed that not even a priest mouth-farting the national anthem of Hungary could stir them from their boredom.

As Father Frank babbled on, I briefly wondered if this would be the moment where I fell writhing to the ground, spewing brilliant green vomit onto the asbestos. Part of me couldn't believe the ridiculousness of the performance or the fact that I was meant to play along, subservient and awed. More than that, though, I felt overcome by a profound defensiveness: *I can't let anyone think I believe this.*

I'm not sure how long it went on—maybe ten seconds, maybe a minute—before I made the mistake of locking eyes with Sonja. She clenched her teeth and pulled back her jaw like you do when you've just seen someone do something really embarrassing.

I couldn't help it. I let out a loud, curt yelp of laughter. It shot through the room like I bullet. I slapped my hands to my mouth.

Father Frank stopped midstream. His grip on my skull

weakened. His fingers brushed the skin of my neck like in the schoolyard game where someone pretends to crack an egg on your head and the yolk runs down and down. My scalp prickled in his absence. I returned my gaze to my clasped hands, my face pulsing with heat. I could feel something hot emanating off Father Frank too. I couldn't tell if it was because a student had disrespected him, because his ancient holy ritual had been interrupted, or because his ruse had been revealed, but I sensed it, the way the often ashamed can easily detect shame in others. Maybe he was angry, or maybe he was just sad.

"Alright, Marly," he said with a sigh. There were a few awkward giggles, but mostly there was silence. "You can go back to your seat."

I kept my eyes glued to the floor. Even as the class shifted to a lackluster discussion of Acts 2, I sat in the back of the room unable to focus on anything but the black pit of regret bubbling in my stomach. My head spun.

After class, Patrick McCormick zoomed up to me for a high five.

"Dude!" he said, wreaking of sweat and body spray. "That was crazy!"

I tepidly returned the high five. I couldn't slake the searing guilt burning in my chest. My laughter had at first seemed like an insurrectionary act of defiance, a bold refusal to play along with the silly old priest and his dramatic game. Now, it felt like a gross betrayal.

At home that evening, as I looked at my mother's whisp of a ponytail and her slow, pained movements over the stove, I feared I had squandered my one and only opportunity to save her. In the following two years, I would think about this moment often: how I'd had the chance to call upon divine grace, and all I'd done was sit there, self-conscious and confused, and laugh.

•

The church doesn't hand out exorcisms like Communion. This is essentially what Father Karras tells Chris MacNeil when he meets with her at the Key Bridge walkway one afternoon not long after Regan masturbates with the crucifix and punches her mother in the face. If Chris wants an exorcism for her daughter, Karras tells her, she might as well hop into a time machine and travel back to the sixteenth century. It just doesn't happen anymore, he says, "not since we learned about mental illness, paranoia, schizophrenia." Besides, exorcisms take time. The church would have to conduct a thorough investigation. Karras would be expected to provide them with tangible proof of possession, such as Regan speaking in a foreign language or knowing things a twelve-year-old girl couldn't possibly know. Karras tells Chris that the chances of the church approving an exorcism are very, very slim. But when Chris breaks down crying on his shoulder, Karras agrees to come take a look anyway.

Karras visits Regan several times before he is willing to accept that she is indeed possessed. He is a serious man, after all, a Jesuit with an advanced degree in psychiatry. He is a man who believes in medicine and science, though these days he's starting to doubt medicine and science too. These days, Karras is getting dangerously close to believing in nothing at all. Even when Regan taunts him about his dead mother and sends dresser drawers flying across the room and projectile vomits green slime all over his sweater, Karras continues to doubt. It is only when the words *Help me* appear on Regan's stone-cold stomach, as if etched from the inside, that Karras agrees to seek help from the higher-ups.

First, he meets with an unnamed priest whom he simply calls "your excellency." Later, that priest meets with another priest in a wood-paneled room decorated with dozens of seemingly identical paintings of Catholic cardinals. In the center of the room sits a long oak table lined with red leather chairs. It's the kind of room that makes you wonder what other conversations have happened there, what other things these men have discussed, or planned to hide.

After weighing the pros and the cons, the two priests decide to move forward with the exorcism of Regan MacNeil.

To assist Karras, they call in Lankester Merrin, an elderly priest who once performed an exorcism in Africa that lasted for months.

•

Near the end of high school, I diverted my acceptance to the University of Oregon and convinced my parents to let me spend a year studying at a historic university in Salamanca, Spain. Growing up, my mother had often told me of her dream for me: that I would go to college at the Catholic university in town, major in nursing or education, and then move into the yellow farmhouse down the street with my husband and twins. Imagine her disappointment when I announced with self-congratulatory pride that I wanted to fly away to the Iberian Peninsula, study the poems of Federico García Lorca, and probably never marry a man or give birth to a single child, let alone two at once.

"Sometimes it is better to live a quiet life at home," my mother counseled.

I, of course, did not agree. As soon as I'd gotten the idea of going away to Spain, sunbaked land of flamenco and ham, the thought of spending the next four years in rainy, Pabst-soaked Eugene was unbearable. I wanted my earth soaked in Rioja wine. One afternoon, after my parents had denied my request yet again, I ran up to my bedroom in angry tears.

"You are condemning me to a life of mediocrity!" I screamed down the stairwell before slamming my door with such melodramatic force it sent the framed William Stafford poems that lined our hallway swaying.

Eventually, they relented. I was able to convince them after providing financial proof that the cost of one year at a university in Europe was the same as studying at a state school for a year, not, of course, including the spending money I'd need to take spiritually and intellectually enriching weekend trips to places like Lisbon and Paris. Self-discovery, I argued, was priceless.

The entire summer preceding my departure, my mother spent sobbing. She cried at my graduation, where I had once again burst into inappropriate laughter when the tiny, overly tanned vice principal recited the entire text of Bob Dylan's "Forever Young" as if she had written it herself. She cried at the grocery store and at the bank and at the mall where we went to buy sturdy walking shoes for my endless European wanderings. She cried at Benihana on my eighteenth birthday, and she cried as I packed my giant suitcase the day before my flight, telling me again and again that I didn't have to leave, that I should be a normal child and stay. She cried on the drive to the airport the next morning, and she cried hardest of all as she hugged me tight before I disappeared through airport security and didn't bother to look back.

Salamanca was a city that literally glowed; it was constructed entirely of golden sandstones that burned bright in the night. On one stone wall of the university, you could still see faded red lines from where students in the fourteenth century had signed their names in bull's blood after finals. It was a college town like Eugene, but instead of Trev's and Jimmy's and the Keg, it had La Chupiteria and Camelot and Cum Laude. Instead of a drizzly quad, it had the baroque Plaza Mayor, where you could drink café cortados and eat olives in the sun. Instead of boys named Zach and Josh and Andrew, it had boys named Javier and Fernando and Rafael. On the weekends, Madrid was just a two-hour bus ride away.

On my first night in Spain, I went out drinking in Madrid with two other American girls, college students studying abroad their junior year. Strangely enough, we were all redheads, and the three of us staggering around the cobblestone streets was apparently quite the sight to behold. Near the end of the night, we met a handsome band of Germans at a crowded bar. They were tall and strapping and blond. Drunk off travel and watered-down well vodka, I was ready to dive into my first European lovefest with a man named Klaus. Klaus was animated and friendly, and he shared my affection for the German techno song titled "Disco Pogo." I was about to make a move when one of his friends turned to him and whispered a single word into his hear: *kirsche.*

"What does that mean?" I asked Klaus.

"Nothing," he said.

I pressed.

"Cherry," he said, finally relenting, shaking his head and preparing to walk away. "It means you're too young."

Klaus's friend was right. I was young, so young, but I didn't feel that way: I felt brazen and capacious and wise. Like most naïve Americans who study abroad, I wanted to experience everything and return home in a year, changed. I took the train to Granada and watched the sun set over the snow-dusted Sierra Nevada. I took the train to Lisbon, got caught in a flash flood, and spent a drizzly Halloween eating weed brownies and going to an S&M club with three Portuguese boys whose names I don't remember. My Spanish literature teacher was a middle-aged man with rotting teeth who nonetheless sent all the women of the class swooning when he recited "Si Mis Manos Pudieran Deshojar" from memory. I let random men shove their hands down my pants in La Chupiteria and Camelot and Cum Laude. I stayed up until 5:00 a.m. most Friday nights and passed out alone in bed with warm churros flaking inside my jacket pockets.

One such night, I met a sandy-haired boy with a mole on his cheek who introduced himself as Pablo and promptly professed his love to me. By our third drink together, he'd offered to take me on a road trip through Galicia, where he was born. It was like something out of *Vicky Cristina Barcelona*, I thought, a movie I'd watched that summer and mistaken for the height of art house cinema. We would eat fresh shellfish and drink crisp Albariño wines, Pablo said. We would hike the Camino de Santiago and wander through the great arches at Praia das Catedrais, he said. That we would make love, he didn't say, but it was implied, and I was thrilled. When we parted ways at the end of the night, I gave him my number and stumbled back to my residencia, giddy with the promise of European romance.

The next morning, I received a stern call from my mother informing me that she'd spent the last several hours fielding calls from a passionate Spaniard demanding that she put me on the line. Like a punch to the gut, I realized that I had drunkenly given Pablo my old home phone number instead of the new one for my reloadable Spanish cell. "Marlena! Marlena!" he'd apparently cried out to my very annoyed mother. "Why have you forsaken me?" Needless to say, I never got my Gallaecian romance.

For the first two months of my trip, my mother called me almost every day, overage charges be damned. We would talk for maybe five minutes, her voice gentle and strained and far away. Eventually, I told her I couldn't talk to her as often any-more because it was interfering with my "experience." She said she understood.

Still, there was part of me that knew, even before I knew. I lit a candle for her in the cathedral of every city I visited: Bar-celona, Segovia, Cuenca, Seville. The cathedrals of Spain were alight with small flickering flames dedicated to my mother. I didn't pray when I lit them, not exactly. Instead, I wordlessly intoned something noncommittal and vague, like "For Mom." I had stopped believing in God or miracles, but I believed in something enough to light a candle and quietly hope it made a difference from an ocean and continent away.

I returned home to Portland that Christmas for what I thought was going to be a quick ten days. When I reached the arrivals gate at PDX, I searched for my mother but saw only my dad and brother. My dad handed me a bouquet of flowers and matter-of-factly told me that my mother had spent all day at the hospital and was waiting for me at home. As we drove back to the suburbs over the Marquam Bridge, I was too dis-tracted to appreciate the blinking city skyline I'd been secretly missing for months.

"Is that my baby girl?" my mother called from the top of the staircase when I opened the front door to the house, our dachshunds, Miles and Danny, yipping at my feet.

She emerged from her bedroom in a purple turtleneck sweater and striped pajama pants that hung off her bone-thin legs. Her hair had gone splotchy and gray, receding up her forehead like an ocean tide. As I began walking up the stairs toward her, I noticed that the turtleneck was unsuccessfully hiding a large lump swelling at her neck. The lump was red and taut, as if a baseball was straining against her soft skin, trying to break through and fly away: a tumor, blocking the blood flow to her once-slender right arm. Her arm was now puffy and bloated and too white, like something that didn't belong to her. Even her right hand had grown inflamed, like the gloved hand of a cartoon clown. She'd always loved her hands, especially her fingers, how arched and delicate and slim they were.

We met halfway up the staircase and embraced. Her body felt so comforting and soft I could have cried.

"My little mouse," she said.

I knew then that I would not be returning to Spain in January like I'd planned. Instead, I got a part-time job at a beverage distributorship in town, where I spent my days checking in truck drivers and counting up the cash to make sure they hadn't pocketed anything, which they never had. I worked Monday, Wednesday, and Thursday, and spent the rest of the days at home with my mom while my dad was at work and my brother was at school. All of my friends were away at college, and so I kept myself company with movies, choosing titles I thought would turn me into a worldly sophisticate without ever having to leave my basement. I almost convinced myself that watching *L'Avventura* and *Summer with Monika* and *Tokyo Story* was as good as traveling to Italy and Sweden and Japan. Sometimes my mother would watch these movies with me in bed, but she would almost always fall asleep by the end of them. What I didn't tell her was that I would often fall asleep too. Most of the time, I read alone in my room while she watched TV alone: *Keeping Up with the Kardashians* and *House Hunters* and some horrible show called *The Swan,* in which women competed for plastic surgeries, screaming at each other through faces wrapped in bloody gauze. Even though it would have meant keeping her company, I couldn't bring myself to watch these shows with her. It would have tainted my frenzied intellectual project. I considered it a waste of my precious time.

Several days a week, Father Dan came over to the house to say the rosary with her or to deliver the Eucharist. Father Dan reminded me of a youth pastor. Though he didn't play the acoustic guitar, he looked like he should have. He wore forest green sweaters over his clerical collar, a Bible always crooked under one arm. I resented his presence in our house entirely. I didn't like that he was penetrating our gloomy solitude, pretending to deliver absolution but not. One day I found a prayer card he'd left by my mother's bedside table instructing her to see her suffering as a way to better understand Christ's sacrifice. After that, I would eye Father Dan suspiciously whenever we passed on the staircase. My hellos were always curt and half-hearted. I wanted him to know that I saw him as an intruder, a fake.

Still, I felt drawn to my mother's room whenever Father Dan was in the house. I would linger at the doorway, listening to their conversations and prayers. My mother told him that she woke up every morning terrified that this would be the day that she died. She told him how scared she was of being left alone, of the constant sensation she had that everyone in our family was packing their bags and preparing to go someplace very far away from her. She told him that our dogs were the only people that kept her company anymore. She told him she did not want to die, that she was afraid. Father Dan would nod and explain that it was all part of God's plan for her, his marvelous and brilliant plan.

One afternoon, Father Dan noticed me lingering in the doorway. I jumped back and started backpedaling down the hall, but it was too late.

"Marly," he said, kind but firm. "Come pray with us."

Fuck, I thought. I peeked back inside the room. My mother

was lying in bed with her head on a pillow. She gave me a faint, strained smile. *Fuck,* I thought again.

I walked inside and took a seat next to Father Dan. I smiled curtly. My mother looked so small in her bed. She wore a pair of hot-pink pajamas with prints of brown dachshunds all over them. Her right eye had clouded over, rolling like a beautiful marble in its hollow socket. Her skin had taken on an ashen pallor, and her cheeks looked like she was sucking them in. Her gray hair was newborn soft.

Father Dan nodded and opened his Bible to a page marked with gold ribbon. He began reading Psalm 23.

"The Lord is my Shepherd; there is nothing I lack," he said.

I wanted to scoff. *Inspired choice.*

"In green pastures he makes me lie down," read Father Dan. "To still waters he leads me; he restores my soul. He guides me along the right paths for the sake of his name."

I struggled to listen along. All I could think about was the scene in *Titanic* where the priest recites Psalm 23 while screeching sinners go flying off the deck of the ship and into the Atlantic. *Couldn't Father Dan have picked something a little more original?* I thought.

"Even though I walk through the valley of the shadow of death, I will fear no evil, for you are with me," he said. "Your rod and staff comfort me."

Why is Father Dan talking to my dying mother about rods and staffs? I was annoyed—at his choice of scripture, that he was forcing me to listen to it, and most of all, that it was making me cry.

During the lonely months leading up to my mother's death, I never believed in God less or wanted him to exist more. I was certain that death was something finite, a sharp and simple termination of living. All that remained after it was nothing. But I desperately wanted to believe that the dead watch over us, that they are close. I wanted to believe in heaven, a glorious and pain-free place where my mother would go after death and where I would meet her again one day. I tried to believe it, getting on my knees and praying deep into the night, but I couldn't. It was all so improbable and absurd: a lie for weak, scared people that couldn't handle the truth. I was weak and scared, but I told myself I could handle the painful truth. It was under my roof. It had a distinct smell. It watched TV alone.

The tears welled in my eyes. My mother was crying too. I thought of the time she had dropped me off for confirmation class and I'd told her, so firmly and confidently, that God wasn't real. I wished I could fly back in time and take it back, not because I was suddenly convinced otherwise but because I understood that she needed me to believe, that believing was something I could do for her.

Father Dan was so kind. He had come and sat with my mother when I wouldn't, and perhaps that was why he called me in: not because I believed but because he saw the power in these rituals. They did what you wanted them to do. I closed my eyes. I thought of the candles I'd lit for her all over Spain, flickering uselessly in tourist-clogged churches.

"You anoint my head with oil," Father Dan continued. "My cup overflows. Indeed, goodness and mercy will pursue me all the days of my life; I will dwell in the house of the Lord for endless days."

He finished and closed the Bible, securing the thin gold ribbon between its pages. The three of us sat there in silence.

"Thank you, Father," my mother finally managed. Her voice cracked in her throat.

"Yeah," I said, suddenly embarrassed. "Thanks."

I stood up and headed out of the room. I didn't want either of them to see my tears, though I suppose they already had.

A few days later, I was sitting by mother's bed reading

Anna Karenina—another attempt to become worldly and profound—when she suddenly sat upright. I hadn't seen her move that swiftly in months. She held up her arms and seemed to run her fingers through a film of invisible cobwebs. She looked transfixed, slightly captivated, and then just confused.

"Marly," she asked. "What's this?"

I put down my book and looked at her for a few moments, trying to see what she saw.

"Mom, there's nothing there," I eventually said.

She lowered her hands back down as if she had been sharply denied. I wondered if perhaps she wanted to show me something. I knew it was just the loads of painkillers she was on, but part of me hoped she was on the precipice of another reality, seeing through to the place that would soon welcome her. I wanted it so badly for her. I remember praying then that she wasn't afraid in that moment but amazed, that she was seeing part of the green valley and clear rushing waters that Father Dan said awaited her, and that it was beautiful and welcoming and good.

From there, things devolved quickly. Our lives continued on like this until she died, with each day worse than the one that came before. It defied my understanding, how brutal and nightmarish death could be. How relentless.

•

Director William Friedkin cut a scene from the original 1973 version of *The Exorcist* that novelist and screenwriter William Peter Blatty considered the spiritual heart of the film. In it, Father Karras and Father Merrin sit in the darkened stairwell just outside of Regan's room, the light from the window above casting bars of shadow across their faces. The exorcism has not been going well. Karras and Merrin have just spent however long dodging massive wads of phlegm and listening to the devil taunt them with homophobic and sacrilegious slurs. Cupboards have been rattling as in an earthquake. Bedside table drawers have flown open for no reason at all. At one point, Regan's body levitated above the bed in a moment of almost startling and sublime beauty. As a viewer, you feel awe in that moment, that perhaps there is something beautiful in what the devil can do. But then her body returns to the bed, and she is back to vomiting and wheezing and shaking her head back and forth on the pillow. Her eyes roll back in her head so you can see only the whites. Regan is far away. It is almost like she is not there at all.

"Father, what's going on here?" asks Father Karras, his voice trembling. He is exhausted and terrified. He can't believe what he has seen and all that there is left to do. "If that's the devil, why this girl? It makes no sense."

Father Merrin sighs and rubs his eyes.

"I think the point is to make us despair, Damien," he responds wearily. "To see ourselves as animal and ugly. To reject our humanity. To reject the possibility that God could ever love us."

Friedkin cut the exchange because he found it too didactic. He wanted his film cleansed of any religious agenda, anything that held the potential to inspire or convert. To explain things, he reasoned, would cheapen the experience for filmgoers, like the scene at the end of *Psycho* when Norman Bates lucidly explains his madness rather than leaving viewers haunted by the question as they file out of the theaters and back into their lives. Friedkin wanted to unsettle his viewers with the nagging mystery of the unknown.

Blatty, on the other hand, believed the film needed this scene, and he fought until the bitter end to keep it in the original cut. Blatty told Mark Kermode that this scene allowed viewers "to understand why you were being subjected to all this horror, why the girl was suffering, why everyone in the film was enduring so much." To Blatty, the horror was a vehicle for a powerful message. The cut scene between Karras and Merrin offered audiences the assurance that everything in the film, as in life, happens for a grander reason than to simply terrify and degrade. Blatty wanted to tell us that despite all the pain and suffering and filth of life on earth, each of us is endowed with an immaculate and endless light.

The jury is still out on whether this scene makes the 2000 rerelease any better than the original. I don't mind it, but I don't think it holds quite the weight that Blatty thinks it does. Blatty has often repeated his belief that *The Exorcist* is a spiritual film because it sends the message that if there are demons, there must be angels as well. This, we are supposed to assume, is what Karras learns by the end of the film. Seeing Regan possessed by the devil affirms his belief in the devil's opposite. But if we are to accept angels in our life, then doesn't that also mean that at any point our life could be overtaken by a horror so brutal and relentless it defies the imagination?

After this conversation, Father Karras takes a break downstairs and talks with Chris. He tells her the exorcism isn't over, but they are close. When he returns to the room, Father Merrin is dead, lying on the floor in a pool of spilled holy water reflecting the light of the moon.

Father Karras then calls the demon out of Regan's body.

"Take me!" he cries. "Come into me!"

The devil does. Karras thrusts himself out the window and falls to his death down the staircase outside.

Father Dyer arrives on the scene minutes later. He asks Father Karras, who is lying face down at the foot of the stairs, if he wants to receive his last rites.

Karras squeezes his hand back as if to say, *Yes, yes, I want to receive them.*

•

Father Allen presided over my mother's funeral. Though the ceremony was held at Sacred Trinity, Father Dan's terrain, Father Allen had insisted. He was a Jesuit, after all. Why wouldn't we want a Jesuit at my mother's funeral? Father Dan respectfully agreed to provide backup.

As Father Allen stood on the altar delivering the mass, I was reminded of the time Sonja and I giggled in the darkened retreat hallway as he asked rows of nervous high school students whether or not they ever touched themselves.

I hated the funeral, the dour performance of it. I sensed people watching me, sussing up the show. When it came time to receive the Communion, I stayed stubbornly planted in the front pew with my dad. I had no intention of taking part in a sacrament I no longer believed in. Father Allen noticed I had not stood up and, assuming that I was too overcome by grief to move, walked over and delivered the Communion wafer directly into my palm. My upper lip curled at the presumption of it. At the same time, I found something naive and sweet in the gesture too: that he thought I'd still find comfort in Communion or that I had any use for belief.

I eyed the pale wafer in my palm. People were staring. My aunts and uncles. My mother's friends. People from the parish I hadn't seen in years. I placed the wafer into my dry mouth and swallowed. I'd been crying for days, and my throat felt sore, clenched. My tongue was a grooved piece of bark in my mouth. It was as if all the moisture had leeched from my body. I couldn't summon enough saliva to properly force the wafer down. It scratched along my esophagus and stayed lodged there for the rest of the mass, never quite dissolving.

•

In the final scene of *The Exorcist,* Father Dyer visits the house on 3600 Prospect Street to see Chris and Regan off before they leave DC for good. He is wearing his clerical collar and a jacket. Chris tells Father Dyer that Regan remembers nothing of her possession, which they both consider a blessing.

Regan emerges from the house wearing a knit hat and a heavy navy coat. You can see faint bruises on her cheeks, but she looks otherwise healthy, subdued. She smiles at Father Dyer. Her eyes are instantly drawn to the starched white window at his neck. She pauses. Then she stands up on her tippy toes and gives him a quick kiss on the check.

For a brief moment, she looks confused by her actions, unsure of why she did it, or of what strange power compelled her.

•

I have felt the presence of what we might call the divine only once in my life. I was twenty-six and traveling through Chile to visit my friend Natalie, who had recently moved to the south of the country to live with her family in a small town at the foot of a volcano. Before I took the twelve-hour bus ride down Chile's long ribbon of a coast, I spent two days alone in the capital, Santiago. I stayed up late my first night drinking beer at my hostel with a Brazilian man who'd noticed the Clarice Lispector novel I was reading. I don't remember his name, only that he was obsessed with Pearl Jam and amazed when I told him I grew up only a few hours away from Seattle.

The Brazilian and I spent the next morning wandering from atrocity to atrocity at the Museo de la Memoria y los Derechos Humanos before grabbing lunch at a restaurant near the Cerro Santa Lucia and parting ways. I then walked around the colorful streets of Bellavista until I reached the Cerro San Cristóbal, the third highest point in the city. I didn't know anything about the giant hill other than that from the top you could see all of Santiago sprawl out before you and, if you were lucky, catch glimpses of the Andes through the smog. Though you could take a tram to the top, I decided to make the climb.

At the summit, I was surprised to discover a small sanctuary dedicated to the Immaculate Conception, complete with a towering, seventy-two-foot, bright white statue of the Blessed Virgin Mary. I was exhausted from the heat, the jetlag, and the climb. Sweat pooled at the back of my neck. The statue was surrounded by a small amphitheater where people sat to pray. A sound system played swooning instrumental Christian music, not unlike the kind we used to play out of the boombox during Stations of the Cross at the Sacred Trinity.

I gazed up at the glowing statue. I'd always had a soft spot for the Virgin Mary. I sometimes felt that if Catholicism had been based more around her and less around Jesus, I might have been able to get behind it more easily. I think part of it was that my mother's name was also Mary, and so her significance to me as Heavenly Mother was both personal and theological. And it mattered that she was a woman. Without her and her immaculate womb, the entire religion wouldn't exist.

Legs wobbling, I drifted into a small stone chapel at the base of the statue. I hadn't been to church since my mother's funeral. This is where Pope John Paul II had blessed Santiago three years before the end of the Pinochet dictatorship. Inside, the chapel was simple and unadorned, with dark wood pews, brown stone walls, and a fairly basic altar decorated with unassuming bouquets and rather amateurish frescos of the angels and saints. It certainly paled in comparison to other chapels I'd seen around Europe, and yet for some reason, I felt compelled to linger. It was cool and quiet inside, a relief compared to the stifling Santiago heat. There were about five other people there with me, praying or lighting candles near the altar.

As soon as I slid into a middle pew and sat down, I felt it, as sudden and undeniable as a slap to the face. A distinct and unyielding presence filled me up like helium and knocked me back into the seat. The sensation was so overwhelming and intense that I immediately burst into tears. I had never in my life started crying for no discernable reason. I was amazed by it, even as it surprised and unsettled me. I couldn't stop crying, and I couldn't say why. All I knew was that I had felt something I had never felt before, something unknowable reaching out from someplace else to briefly and indelibly make itself known.

People nodded and smiled at me nervously as they walked down the aisle toward the exit. I felt self-conscious about my tears, but I was powerless before them. They just kept coming. Already, I was searching for explanations for what I was feeling: jetlag, dehydration, a slight hangover from my late night listening to the Brazilian sing "Jeremy" in broken English. Nothing quite explained it. Despite my attempts to dismiss or diminish it, I knew that what I was feeling was inexplicable, the type of experience that only happens to those who aren't looking.

I walked back down the *cerro* awash with wellbeing, feeling simultaneously full and drained. I stopped at a small outdoor café in Bellavista for a coffee and drank it while watching the city pass me by. My feeling of serenity promptly ended when a large man in his midforties asked me my age and then, once I was able to affirm that I was legal, quite blatantly asked me if I'd like to go back to his place for a quick fuck. I politely declined. This taught me something too: There is always someone waiting around the corner, ready to smash your spiritual epiphany into pieces.

In Pucón, I told Natalie about the experience. We had just finished a hike at the Santuario El Cañi, a nature preserve offering pristine views of the snow-dusted Villarrica volcano, and were sitting on a log near a clear blue lake surrounded by Araucaria trees.

"It was probably just exhaustion," I said. "Or a small seizure."

"Maybe," Natalie said. "Or maybe it was your mom."

I wasn't surprised to hear this from Natalie, my most spiritual friend. Natalie considers herself an indigo child—a person with heightened empathetic and supernatural abilities—and she once walked into my apartment in Portland and immediately gasped, "I can feel your mother in here," gesturing toward the old white loveseat that my mother had bought for her first apartment during nursing school. If anyone was going to suggest that my strange feeling in the chapel was evidence of my mother attempting to reach out from the beyond, it was Natalie. Still, I was glad she'd said it. I'd been too afraid to admit that I'd had the same exact thought.

"Yeah," I replied. "Maybe."

I flew back to Portland five days later. The experience did not transform me into a spiritual or devout person. I still have not been to church since my mother's funeral, and I will probably never return. What lingering spirituality I have is rather knee-jerk and embarrassing, like when I accidently say "amen" at the end of yoga class instead of "namaste." And yet the afternoon in Santiago opened something in me that for years had been firmly shut. I still feel like an atheist most days, strongly tethered to my own steadfast disbelief, but when I think of that moment in the Chilean chapel, everything is cast into doubt—luminous and unshakeable doubt.

Part 4

✛

LAYING HANDS ON
THE POSSESSED

THE OPERATING THEATER

Five years after my mother died, I flew to London to visit a friend. Near the end of the trip, I took the train to Edinburgh and spent a drizzly weekend wandering the city alone. I eventually drifted to the Scottish National Portrait Gallery, where I passed through hall after hall filled with paintings of lords, labor politicians, and ladies of high society. By the third floor, my mind had strayed. I was ready to reenter the damp streets in search of a late lunch when I almost walked straight into a painting called *Three Oncologists* by the Scottish artist Ken Currie.

In the painting, three male surgeons gather around a curtain that opens up into the darkened abyss of an operating theater. Their bodies blur at the edges. Their faces glow eerily as if haunted, or haunting. The figures appear closer to luminous apparitions than real people, though each of them represents a pioneer in the field of oncology: Dr. Alfred Cuschieri, Dr. David Lane, and Dr. Robert Steele. Currie portrays each man in mid-action. One holds up his blood-covered hands. Another brandishes a gleaming medical instrument. The third clutches some sort of document at his side. Their eyes are rimmed with red from exhaustion and perhaps also fear. It is as if the daily toll of performing such brutal surgeries is slowly draining them of their remaining life. Despite this, they are poised to reenter the operating theater and resume their latest attempt to bring the patient out of the darkness and into the light.

The patient, of course, is not seen at all. They exist beyond the curtain, shrouded in the dense black mystery of disease, as if the real story of cancer is not the body it afflicts but the heroic and haunted men who will save that body from affliction.

According to the plaque I read at the painting's side, *Three Oncologists* is meant to express "the sense of horror and anxiety associated with cancer." *But who is experiencing this horror and anxiety?* I wondered. *The doctors? The sick? Society as a whole?* I stood in front of the painting for nearly twenty minutes, my hunger completely forgotten. I couldn't stop looking at the faint curtain that looms in the painting's background, so much like the curtains at the theater or the cinema. I could easily imagine the doctors turning and stepping past it onto the medical stage, confident that this performance, this barbaric ritual of faith, will be the one that saves a life.

Compare *Three Oncologists,* painted in 2002, to *The Agnew Clinic,* painted in 1889 by American artist Thomas Eakins. *The Agnew Clinic* takes viewers inside the operating theater, where rows of young male medical students in suits watch as four male doctors in white coats perform a radical mastectomy on a woman who lies prone and exposed in the center of the room. Doctor David Hayes Agnew stands off to the side of the operating table, gesticulating and lecturing to the crowd. There is something performative in Agnew's stance, as if he is there to entertain first, educate second, heal third.

In operating theaters of the past, doctors were indeed known to ham it up for the crowds, which were often made up of not just medical students and professors but hospital administrators, employees, family members of the patient, and even wealthy patrons who paid to see these operations performed

live, often bringing bacteria and viruses into the operating theater along with them. This type of public operation gained
popularity after the 1840s, when the increasing use of anesthesia made it palatable to watch the procedures without having
to hear the blood-curdling screams of the patients as doctors
dug into their flesh with scalpels. The patient, once excruciatingly conscious, was now blessedly reduced to an unconscious
body on the operating table.

Eakins's commitment to scientific realism was such that
almost every person depicted in the painting represents a real
person enrolled at or employed by the University of Pennsylvania School of Medicine. In certain reproductions of the
painting online, you can scroll over each of the students in
the audience and find out their real names. Their faces show
an intriguing variety of reactions to the procedure: grave, serious, fascinated, disgusted, bored. A few turn to each other and
leer, as if they are more interested in the bare breasts exposed
on the operating table than the procedure they are expected to
learn.

Eakins's lauded realism ended at the female body, however. The patient on the operating table is the only person in
the painting who does not represent a real human. When you
hover the cursor over her body online, no name appears. The
woman is, in more ways than one, a pure invention. In the
days before mammograms and self-examinations, the tumor in
a woman's breast would likely have grown large and increasingly painful by the time she visited a doctor to seek treatment. The tumor on the breast was often accompanied by raw,
ulcerated skin and blood leaking from the nipples. In especially
advanced cases, the flesh would necrotize, leaving the chest
muscles and the ribcage exposed.

Eakins instead chose to paint a young, unblemished breast.
While nineteenth-century decorum typically required the wom-

an's entire body to be covered by a medical sheet, leaving only her cancerous breast visible, in Eakin's rendering, her entire upper half is bare and available for male study. Aside from the patient, the only other woman in the painting is identified as nurse Mary V. Clymer, who seems to look down at the helpless woman with sympathy or, at the very least, recognition.

Eakins's decision to portray a nude woman undergoing a radical mastectomy was not without its controversy. The painting seemed designed to titillate even as it was meant to capture and instruct. *The Agnew Clinic* was rejected for exhibition at the Pennsylvania Academy of Fine Arts and New York's Society of American Artists. Despite backlash when it finally appeared at the Chicago World's Fair in 1893, *The Agnew Clinic* was heralded as a landmark of scientific advancement, on par with Eadweard Muybridge's zoopraxiscope and Joseph Silsbee's moving walkway. It offered a glimpse into a future where science and technology could overcome even the most ancient and feared of human weaknesses. *The Agnew Clinic* inspired with its depiction of brilliant male surgeons contesting the evil lurking within female flesh and doing so with such expertise that her outward appearance of feminine perfection remained intact.

Eakins had faced simultaneous backlash and acclaim for his medical paintings before. Thirteen years earlier, his painting *The Gross Clinic* had caused a stir when it was exhibited at Ward One of the US Army Post Hospital after once again failing to gain acceptance into other more elite art institutions. The painting depicts another surgeon, Dr. Samuel Gross, presiding over bone surgery before a group of students at Jefferson Medical College. This time, we see only the back of the patient's pale thigh and a thin strip of red on the skin where the doctors have made an incision. Gross brandishes a glinting scalpel in his bloody hand.

Though the painting's execution was widely considered masterful, many were appalled by its gruesome and unpainterly subject matter. A *New York Times* critic called it "so dreadful that the public may well be excused if it turns away in horror."

•

Audience reactions to *The Exorcist* are the stuff of legend: vomiting, seizures, panic attacks, miscarriages, heart failure. Go see *The Exorcist,* and you might leave in a stretcher, or at least that is what the media blitz surrounding the film led people to believe. Many theaters kept smelling salts on hand to reawaken any audience members who might faint during the screenings. Others played it safe and cued up ambulances in advance. These stories became self-fulfilling prophecies, augmenting audience fears before they even stepped foot into the darkened theater. The energy around *The Exorcist* was so palpable that viewers were all but guaranteed to react. I can imagine seeing *The Exorcist* in 1973 and feeling a little bit disappointed if someone in the audience didn't go into cardiac arrest or, at the very least, puke.

In his book *Dark Dreams 2.0: A Psychological History of the Modern Horror Film from the 1950s to the Twenty-First Century,* Charles Derry writes,

> In an era when acts of violence—in the form of killings in Vietnam, live riots, and assassinations—were watched daily over long periods on the evening news, and our responses to death had become complacent and anesthetized, going to *The Exorcist* and throwing up reaffirmed our ability to be revolted, our ability to feel; thus the vomit of the spectators became a valid aesthetic response to the world around them.

Numbness is perhaps a natural and unavoidable reaction to the daily onslaught of war, political corruption, and racial injustice. Derry argues that through the ritual and communal experience of viewing *The Exorcist* in the darkened theater, audience members were given a space to physically react not only to the horror unfolding onscreen but to the apparent chaos engulfing the world outside the cinema doors.

If you haven't seen *The Exorcist*, or you haven't seen it in a while, you might make certain assumptions about what scenes provoked these dramatic audience reactions: Regan's head spinning around on her neck, Regan stabbing herself with a bloody crucifix, Regan projectile vomiting all over those priests. These are the types of scenes you don't need to see to understand. It seems obvious that audiences were so terrified and disgusted by the monstrosity unfolding on screen that they momentarily lost control of their faculties. Their bodies rebelled against what their eyes were taking in. In many ways, *The Exorcist* confirmed something that many of us would rather deny: Human beings are capable of great horrors, there is great evil afoot in the world, and that evil resides in each of us.

In this case, however, the most obvious explanation isn't exactly the right one. The point in *The Exorcist* at which many people started to vomit and faint and generally lose control was not in fact during any of the head-spinning, crucifix-defiling, God-defaming scenes of terror and sacrilege we've come to associate with *The Exorcist*. In fact, it happened well before any of the hardcore possession stuff even begins to kick in.

It happened during the cerebral angiography.

The first half of *The Exorcist* functions much like a traditional illness narrative: a person is mysteriously sick and needs to find out why. When Regan starts acting strangely around her twelfth birthday, culminating in an iconic pissing incident at a fancy dinner party, Chris takes Regan to the doctor for a series of routine examinations. Regan's early symptoms manifest themselves more as standard teen angst than demonic possession. In the examination room, she hums to herself and sways like a hippie at Woodstock. When a nurse takes her reflexes, Regan responds in a dull monotone, "I don't feel anything."

Though Regan is prone to lying and swearing, it at first seems as if there is nothing seriously wrong with her. The doctor diagnoses it as a "disorder of the nerves" brought on by an overreaction to depression, and he prescribes Ritalin. When Regan's misbehavior worsens—spitting on doctors, calling them bastards, punching them in the face—her doctor suspects a "disturbance in the chemical electrical activity of the brain's temporal lobe" and prescribes Thorazine. Eventually, when neither the Thorazine nor the Ritalin succeed in curbing Regan's volatile symptoms, the doctor calls for a more rigorous and invasive series of tests, including a spinal tap, a pneumoencephalography, and the infamously vomit-inducing cerebral angiography.

During the offending scene, Regan lays down on an examination table, her lips chapped and her skin drained of all color. She rests atop a crude brown medical pad. Her naked body is covered with a thin blue sheet. The room itself is a dull wash of browns and beiges—it doesn't gleam in the way that decades of watching medical dramas have taught me to expect. A team of male radiologists gather around Regan. One of them lowers the top of her gown and attaches wires to her bare shoulders. He paints her pale, supple neck with a cool liquid that makes her quiver at the touch. "Very sticky," one radiologist says in a kind, calming tone.

Another doctor then pierces the spot on her neck with a frighteningly long needle. Regan winces as a bright red shot of blood spurts out of her neck. She yelps, keeping her eyes shut tight. A skinny tube is slowly inserted into her neck, narrowing the flow of blood into a transparent channel that stretches off the screen. The radiologists place duct tape across her forehead and chin to keep her from shifting about during the procedure. A big, bulky device then hovers over Regan's body to take the X-rays. It hums like a copier and begins to clack oppressively, as if it is shooting invisible bullets into Regan's skull. Chris watches from a window in the observation room above, holding her fingers to her lips.

The scene has the faint air of Inquisitional torture, as powerful men wield sharp, vaguely gothic instruments in an attempt to expunge evil from the body of a sinning woman. It is a scene all too open to symbolic interpretation: erect syringes penetrating prone female flesh, the orgasmic shots of blood, the wincing and the moans. As Mark Kermode writes, "It would be difficult to present a more brutal, hopeless, and even pornographic depiction of modern medicine." Even screenwriter William Peter Blatty admits that he had to turn away during the scene.

He tells a story about watching it in a theater as the woman seated in front of him repeatedly muttered "Jesus" under her breath.

"I hope that's not Pauline Kael," he claims to have thought to himself.

Though *The Exorcist* does not show the full procedure, medical professionals praised the scene for its accuracy, an accuracy achieved in part by the presence of a real radiographer. In 1972, while scouting locations and extras for *The Exorcist*, Friedkin visited the New York University Medical Center and watched a young man named Paul Bateson perform a live cerebral angiography. Friedkin was so impressed with Bateson's professionalism and sense of style—he apparently wore an earring and a leather bracelet to work—that he cast him in the film. Four years after the premier of *The*

Exorcist, Bateson was convicted of murdering *Variety* reporter Addison Verrill and charged with the murders of several other gay men throughout Greenwich Village, whose dismembered bodies were found floating in medical bags in the East River. Bateson would inspire Friedkin's controversial later film *Cruising,* about a cop played by Al Pacino who goes undercover in New York's leather scene to catch a sadistic killer.

Bateson's post-*Exorcist* history certainly lends a retrospective chill to the scene, but the audiences who saw the film in the early 1970s knew nothing about Bateson or what he would later do. They were reacting solely to the film's graphic depiction of a painful and, in Kermode's words, "hopeless" medical procedure. Hopeless, in this case, because it is ultimately futile. In the following scene, the doctors examine Regan's X-rays and shake their heads.

"There's nothing there," they say, baffled.

When such medical interventions fail to reveal the root of Regan's illness, she is sent to a psychiatrist, a hypnotist, and a state-of-the-art research facility called the Barringer Clinic. In this way, *The Exorcist* is really a tale of misdiagnosis. Regan is a perfect cinematic representation of the pathological female body, a degraded version of the female ideal violently eluding male medical mastery and control. She is told again and again that nothing is wrong with her, that all her intense and undeniable physical symptoms are nothing but the manifestation of some mental weakness or deficiency. The answer to her ailment continues to escape each medical professional until Regan is essentially prescribed what we might call an extreme form of bedrest: locked alone in a cold room with her limbs bound to the posts of her bed. Despite the excruciating and extreme interventions Regan undergoes throughout *The Exorcist,* traditional medicine is unable to offer her salvation.

Overt sexism aside, *The Exorcist* forces viewers to confront the unwelcome reality that the things meant to save us often cause us indescribable pain and that the people tasked with making us well often falter or fail. Medicine is an ever-evolving, imperfect, and often shockingly barbaric science. Regan's sometimes comic levels of violence toward medical professionals is perhaps a response many of us can relate to. Who among us has not felt occasional disdain for the experts and their pretense of certainty? Who has not felt helpless in the face of their power or cowed by what we allow them to do to our bodies and the bodies of the ones we love? Who has not found themselves wondering if the solution to what ails us lies elsewhere?

The Exorcist is ultimately pessimistic about modern science. In the end, it is neither medicine nor psychology that cures Regan. It is Catholicism. It is not doctors but priests that offer her salvation. Though Chris MacNeil initially mocks the prospect of an exorcism for her sick daughter, she eventually takes refuge in the divine. When all else fails, there is only God. *The Exorcist* enacts a strange and perhaps regressive reversal of humanity's general trend away from occult or spiritual responses to human malady and toward scientific solutions. Whereas the progress of medicine allowed us to say, *No, she is not possessed, she is ill, The Exorcist* insists upon the opposite: *No, she is not ill, she is possessed.*

•

Demonic superstitions about the sick body have swirled around the collective consciousness since antiquity. Especially in the Christian tradition, bodily disease was long viewed as punishment for a life of sin or uncleanliness. Illness was often believed to be the earthly manifestation of the Lord's righteous wrath. What Susan Sontag calls Christianity's "moralized notions of disease" established cancer, one of the most dreaded of all human ailments, either as holy vengeance or as a test of a faith, a way to prove your devotion and reap the heavenly rewards. Centuries of failure to save people from the ravages of cancer served to further cloak the illness in thick layers of misconception, silence, and dread. This shadowy netherworld of medical defeat, public denial, and private suffering transformed cancer into evil incarnate and justified whatever brutal surgical interventions were considered necessary to rid the body of the sinister demon slowly corroding it from within.

After centuries of silence and fear, the 1970s marked a landmark decade for cancer research and awareness. Over the course of several years, the disease emerged from the darkness of taboo and seized the national stage. The moon landing was still fresh in the nation's mind, reminding people of the seemingly endless potential of science and human ingenuity. If man could hurl himself into the stars and touch the moon, then surely man could also conquer the mysterious maladies lurking deep within the inner space of the body. In 1971 alone, the *New York Times* ran over 450 cancer-related articles. That same year, Nixon signed the National Cancer Act, which bolstered the authority of the National Cancer Institute, established fifteen new cancer research centers across the country, and allocated increased funding to cancer research and training. With both the Vietnam War and Watergate consuming public attention, Nixon clung to the idea of a cancer cure as some sort of reputation-saving coup de grâce. If he was the president who cured cancer, Nixon reasoned, then certainly the American people could learn to overlook his many crimes. The disease, once "a sign of divine retribution at work," to borrow Sontag's words, now became a highly visible and highly publicized national priority, a new front on America's ever-expanding list of wars.

Cancer not only became politically visible in the 1970s. It

also began playing a larger role in movies, TV, and literature. Erich Segal's best-selling leukemia romance *Love Story* was published in 1970 and made into a box-office smash starring Ali MacGraw and Ryan O'Neal that same year. My mother once told me that *Love Story* was one of her favorite books. In the sixth grade, when I checked out a molding copy with stained yellow pages from my tiny middle school library, expecting to find a juicy romance in the vein of Judy Blume's *Forever,* I was disappointed that instead of sex, there was only cancer.

Several other cancer books were adapted for the screen throughout the early seventies, including *Bang the Drum Slowly* and *Brian's Song.* In 1972 beloved child star Shirley Temple Black made strides by going public with her cancer diagnosis instead of silently weathering it in private. In 1974 CBS's *The Young and the Restless* broadcast the first ever cancer saga on TV, following the character Jennifer Brooks from diagnosis through treatment and recovery. Cancer became a saga, a slogan, a spectacle to consume.

In *The Emperor of All Maladies: A Biography of Cancer,* Siddhartha Mukherjee writes, "There is, in retrospect, something preformed in [this] magnification [of cancer], a deeper resonance—as if cancer had struck the raw strings of anxiety already vibrating in the public psyche." As Mukherjee notes, we tend to project our own inner conflicts onto the illnesses that capture public attention in certain potent historical moments. It is possible that cancer was amplified in the early 1970s precisely because it "epitomized the internal horror" spreading throughout the United States at the time: fear that our once good and mighty nation was being slowly consumed by something toxic and evil, that it would never be the same. Just as society's anxieties slowly shifted away from the extranational (the atomic bomb, communist armies, space invaders) and toward the domestic (devastated cities, declining morals, and radical youth), so too did horror change, away from movies like *Invasion of the Body Snatchers, The Thing,* and *War of the Worlds* and toward *The Omen, Shivers,* and *The Exorcist.* It makes sense then that Nixon would wage a war against the disease that so perfectly mirrored his entire campaign platform, and that so many filmmakers would seize on possession as a novel and effective way to strike fear into viewers' hearts.

In film after film from the era, a mysterious and maleficent presence invades and corrupts the individual, turning the body—and indeed the soul—into something monstrous and unrecognizable. Viewers looked on in horror as bodies writhed in agony, excreted noxious fluids, and succumbed to some ancient and corrosive evil. Very rarely did the camera step inside these horrific bodies to show viewers what the world looked like from their individual perspective, to show the audience their horror, their desire, their pain, their strength. In the case of *The Exorcist,* the audience is meant to relate to Regan's mother, Chris, who watches her daughter's transformation in horror, and to the male priests who, like surgeons brandishing glinting scalpels in an operating theater, finally arrive with their gleaming crosses to expel the demon from Regan's tortured flesh. Regan's degradation is pure and empty theater, medical Grand Guignol. Audience members are encouraged to watch, to scream, and, when things get too intense, to look away.

The monsters in these films remain dreaded spectacles. The audience is afraid of them at the same time that they fear becoming them.

•

My mother was first diagnosed with breast cancer when I was six years old. Because I was so young, I can recall very little about her illness. I mainly remember the shock of her bald head and the various scarves, hats, and wigs she bought to cover it. These accessories were infinitely amusing to me. I loved plunging my hands into her closet drawers and pulling scarves out in reams, like a magician. Outwardly optimistic, my mother framed the whole thing as a fashion adventure, an opportunity to experiment with daring new looks. I became so obsessed with a particular fuzzy pink bucket hat that my mother eventually relented and gave it to me. She preferred her sandy blond wig anyway. I thought the wig looked strange on her head, which is why I often liked to snatch it away and put it on my own.

In public, however, I was embarrassed by her baldness, vaguely resentful even. People stared. I felt a weird and intense jealousy toward my classmate Nicki, whose mother was young, tan, and pregnant. I would watch her pick Nicki up from school with a barely concealed mixture of hatred and longing. I wanted my mother to be beautiful and glowing and full of life again.

The rest comes to me in disjointed images, brief flashes I struggle to place in time or context. I remember returning dirty casserole dishes to neighbors' front steps and screaming as my father clumsily raked a brush through my knotted curls when my mother was too sick to help out. I remember the puckered red slashes her double mastectomy left on her chest, and how her once soft, auburn hair grew back darker and coarser. I remember the giant basket filled with one thousand Japanese cranes that arrived at our house one day, a present from a church friend who told us that they were meant to bring recovery and good luck. I remember taking a single bright blue crane out of the basket, ferrying it away to my bedroom, and then feeling terrified that I had somehow disrupted their magic.

But mostly I remember the bag of blood.

My mother was alone in her bedroom when I saw it. I'd wandered in just in time to see her shakily raising herself out of bed. At her side, she held a bag filled with something sloshing and dark. It was blood, though I didn't realize it right away. It wasn't red like blood in the movies. It was a dark, brownish pink. Thicker than I would have imagined, more viscous. There was *matter* sloshing around in there. My mother's matter. It looked like you could squish it between your fingers like jelly.

I watched her walk the nine or ten feet from her bed to the bathroom door. She hadn't noticed I was there. The room smelled alien, not like perfume and powdery department store makeup like it usually did, but sour and metallic. I couldn't believe how slowly she was moving. She was hunched over, her movements trembling and strained. Her skin had taken on a strange color, like bruised fruit. I stared. *Why is her blood in a bag and why is she holding it in her hand?* Something in me recoiled, and then I felt guilty for recoiling. It was shocking and surreal. I stood there, the myth of my mother's immaculate perfection broken, until I felt my dad's hand on my shoulder.

"What are you doing in here?" he said. My mother disappeared beyond the bathroom door. "You shouldn't have seen that."

The bag of blood marks one of my earliest and clearest childhood memories, though it took me years to fully understand it. I now know that the bag of blood was likely there to hold fluid draining from her incisions after her double mastectomy and that she was almost certainly in intense and earthshattering pain.

I finally began putting the pieces together years later, when I read *The Cancer Journals* by Audre Lorde. In the book, Lorde describes the days after her mastectomy with a brutal and searing poetry, evoking not one single agony but a vast panoply of them: burns, aches, stabs, pangs, throbs. She writes of waking up to the feeling that her recently removed breast was being squeezed in a vise, and later feeling as if someone was pressing down upon her chest with a hobnailed boot. She describes the ways anesthesia turned her brain to gray mush, how she swam in and out of pain, in and out of sleep, all while the steady gong of *malignant, malignant, malignant* rang ominously in her mind.

"Sometimes," Lorde writes, "despair sweeps across my consciousness like lunar winds across a barren moonscape. Ironshod horses rage back and forth across my every nerve."

Reading Lorde was part of my clumsy and delayed attempt to better understand my mother's experience of cancer treatment and recovery. When I first read the book, I felt an extreme gratitude to Lorde for so viscerally describing how she felt after her mastectomy, for giving flesh and meaning to what I had seen for years as only a spectacle and a shock. Much like viewers of *The Exorcist* who see only the gruesome physical symptoms of Regan's possession—her chapped lips, distant gaze, bloody crotch, and spewing vomit—I saw only the outer manifestations of my mother's disease: her fatigued limbs, her lost hair, her new and different breasts. It took me far longer than I'd like to admit to begin imagining what she might have been feeling inside, to feel and think myself inside her experience instead of gawking like a scared and stupefied voyeur.

Our cultural narratives tend to flatten sick individuals, to define them solely by their illness and whether or not they overcome it. It is frighteningly easy to see a sick person as just a sick person and nothing but, especially when that sick person is your mother, a person wrapped up in your own lifetime's worth of resentments, misconceptions, and depersonalizations. It can take serious work to worry your way into this narrative void. Despite the omnipresence of illness and disease in our world, the culture doesn't encourage the sick to speak openly and honestly about their experiences unless theirs is one of bravery, endurance, and grateful transformation. Sickness is typically portrayed as either melodrama or horror. Mundane reality is often left out because that reality can feel like too much to bear.

To fill this relative vacuum, I've done my research. I've read the books: *A Darker Ribbon, Malignant, The Cancer Journals, The Undying, When Breath Becomes Air, On Being Ill, The Red Devil: To Hell with Cancer—and Back*. I've watched the movies and TV shows: *The Big C, Breaking Bad, Cries & Whispers*. I've dug around in my mother's closet and studied the remains she left behind. There, I once found a pastel-colored medical pamphlet offering guidance on cancer treatment and recovery. In a tone simultaneously clinical and cheery, the pamphlet warned chemotherapy patients that their fingernails might come loose in their beds and recommended using a soft-bristle toothbrush to avoid nicking the gums while brushing. Before I read the pamphlet, I'd never considered these small but excruciating details: loose nails, bleeding gums. In her closet, I also found a sheet of paper titled Mastectomy Preoperative Bathing Instructions, which discouraged the use of lotions, perfumes, or bacteria-loving loofas prior to surgery and explained the proper way to wash one's sick body with a special, presurgical soap. I've tried to imagine how my mother must have felt washing her own body with that special soap, knowing that she would soon wake up to find part of that body gone. I've tried to imagine the way she must have felt years later, her prone body sliding into the dark tube of an MRI machine, fearful that after all the pain and loneliness and fighting, her cancer was back once again. I've tried to imagine how she must have felt when the doctors told her that her suspicions were correct.

Even as I read, imagine, and furiously attempt to understand, I am forced to confront the fact that I am still partaking in a gross kind of spectatorship, studying her suffering for my own edification and elucidation. All of this self-enforced empathy, several decades too late. Even in my most good-hearted and earnest of attempts, my mother remains as silent as an anesthetized body on an operating table. I busy myself stuffing my own thoughts, feelings, assumptions, and fears into her shut and silent mouth.

And I must also admit this: As much as all of this research and imagining is, in part, a project of empathy, it is also a project of self-protection. After all, my mother and I share DNA. The disease that killed her and her mother before that may soon arrive in my own body, and I want to be prepared, though I know nothing will ever prepare me for something I have not yet experienced. Each time I feel an unexpected pang in my breast or wake up after a night of drinking with the stale taste of cigarettes on my breath, a chilly jolt of dread rushes up my spine. *The cancer,* I think. *It's here.* When I stay up late at night trying to imagine what my mother lived through, I am also trying to imagine what I may one day have no choice but to live through myself. Just as I tossed and turned in bed as a young child terrified of *The Exorcist,* I now toss and turn in bed terrified that the disease that came for my mother will soon come for me, and that then, and only then, will I begin to understand.

•

Perhaps more than any other genre, horror plays upon the natural human fear of having one's body invaded, mutilated, humiliated, consumed, and controlled. Bodily degradation is so central to horror that there is an entire subgenre dedicated to it. In body horror, it is the protagonist's body that becomes the Other, the thing to be feared and ultimately destroyed. The body takes brutal revenge upon the individual it contains. The person is left painfully trapped inside their own skin, alienated from their body and yet unable to escape its terrifying reign.

In many body horror films, such as David Cronenberg's *The Fly*, it is the protagonist who finds their formerly healthy and stable body under attack, forcing audience members to feel a de facto kinship with a character who might otherwise revolt, terrify, or confuse them. As played by Jeff Goldblum, Seth Brundle is a likable and fully realized character whom we relate to even as we wince and gag at his monstrous transformation. I feel both sympathy and disgust as Brundle's ears fall from his molting skin, as he plucks his nails from their oozing beds.

What would *The Exorcist* look like if viewers were encouraged to feel for Regan instead of just fear her? How would the power of the film change if viewers were allowed to experience the possession from her perspective instead of from a distance?

Writing about *The Fly*, Charles Derry posits that the central question of the film, and of body horror in general, is "Do we, as humans, have enough compassion to embrace the bodily degradations of others, or will our own revulsion turn us into even greater monsters?" In Derry's view, it is the audience members who are the real monsters, not the characters on the screen. *The Fly* suggests that the real horror in this life is the human beings among us who are too frightened or disgusted by the physical suffering of others to care, the people who see human frailty, illness, hardship, or disability and do nothing but grimace and turn away. It is those people who should make you run screaming into the night. Sometimes the person you should most fear might even be yourself.

FATHER KARRAS
DREAMS OF HIS MOTHER

At night, Father Karras dreams of his dead mother. In his dreams, she slowly emerges from the depths of a New York subway tunnel dressed in black. Karras sees her from a distance and waves. She calls out to him in response, but he can't hear her, and neither can we. Instead, we hear the faded and distorted sounds of a busy streetscape—honking horns, chattering voices—and a barely discernable industrial clanking. Over that, short grunts and a frenzied rasping: perhaps the drunken sounds Karras makes while he sleeps.

Karras runs to his mother through a busy intersection. He is wearing his gray jogging sweats. The scene is intercut with brief flashes of other images we have seen throughout the film: a falling pendant, a ticking clock, black dogs running through the desert.

Before Karras can reach his mother, she turns around and begins her slow descent back down the staircase and toward the city's shaking underground, toward the dark and hissing tunnels that ferry people from one place to the next.

•

In the years following my mother's death, I dreamt of her often, though I suppose you might call what I had nightmares.

204

My dreams were generally tortured in those years—rats crawling through bloody intestines, amputees laughing at me and pointing, velvet curtains—but the ones involving my mother were always especially disturbing.

In one, I come to in a sketchy bathroom with dirty tile floors and a cracked mirror. My mouth is in the most exquisite and searing pain. When I look at my fragmented reflection, I see that my upper and lower lips have been pierced through with long, rusted nails. I know that if I don't remove them, I won't ever be able to speak again. Slowly, I begin pulling out each bloody nail, one by one, and depositing them in the sink. *Clink.* It seems to take hours. Once I'm done, I call my mother to ask her, the former nurse, how to prevent an infection. She picks up on the second ring, tells me how.

In the most common dream I had during those years, I am walking through a dark and shifting wood. I know I am near a body of water because of the mosquitoes and the dampness in the air. A big white moon bursts through the fog, and the black-green pines loom tall around me. I am looking for something, but I have forgotten what until I see my mother emerge from the darkness. The moon has washed her skin a milky white. She glides. At first, it is almost beautiful, ethereal, and I think we might run toward each other and embrace. As I get closer, however, I see that she is sickly and emaciated like right before she died. Her cheeks are hollow, her eye sockets shadowy caves, her legs sharp sticks of bone. She is not in fact moving of her own accord but struggling against some sort of clear plastic wrap, almost like a transparent body bag. She isn't gliding toward me but stumbling, her gait restricted by the bag, her sunken eyes frightened and wide. She is gasping desperately for breath. Each time she does, the plastic bag sucks in and out.

In the dream, I understand that she has risen from the dead

and that if I can only get her out of that plastic casing, she will be alive and well. As I run toward her, she collapses to the ground next to a dumpster. I can hear the sound of the plastic bag sucking in and out as she tries to breath. I'm doing that dream running, like it's through mud up to my thighs or against gale-force winds pushing me back with every step.

I strain against the invisible pressure and stumble to the ground by her prone body. Her eyes bulge large. I rip open the wrap and free her, but it is too late. She has died again, gone back to wherever she came from.

•

The Exorcist is as much about Father Karras's crisis of faith as it is the extreme guilt he suffers after the death of his aging mother. He is wracked by the unshakeable feeling that he could have done more to help her, that he wasn't there when she needed him most, and that it's his fault she is dead.

The night after his mother dies, Father Karras drinks a bottle of scotch with Father Dyer in his tiny dorm room, the pipes whooshing every time someone flushes the toilet on the floor above. Father Karras curls up on his bed in his white undershirt and sweatpants, moaning to Father Dyer, "I should have been there and I wasn't there. I should have been there and I wasn't there." In the book version of *The Exorcist,* William Peter Blatty describes it as "like childhood, this grief." This scene always strikes me as particularly painful and raw. I have said the same thing to myself many times, crying alone in bed at night. *I should have been there and I wasn't there. I should have been there and I wasn't there.* Sometimes, it almost rocks me to sleep.

The guilt I feel about my mother is endless and immense. I spent my twenties twisting in its clutches. I feel guilty that I spent so much of my adolescent years either fighting with her or not speaking to her at all. I feel guilty about the afternoon she asked me to drive her to chemotherapy and I dropped her off in front of the clinic's sliding glass doors instead of going inside with her. I feel guilty that I still do not know even the basics of what her chemotherapy entailed: Were there blankets over the knees? Conversations with other patients? Something about ringing a bell? I feel guilty that I left for Spain after high school graduation instead of attending a local college like she wanted. I feel guilty about how much I didn't notice or care to understand.

I feel guilty that I took a job during her final months instead of spending every moment of every day keeping her company. I feel guilty that I didn't do more to help her find beauty and goodness in those final days: surrounding her with rare flowers, showing her old photos to remind her of the good times, massaging sweet smelling lotion into her cracked feet. I feel guilty about the time I was helping her drink a glass of water and it slipped from my hand, spilling all over her chest. I feel guilty about the way her eyes widened in shock and she leapt out of bed with a quickness and urgency I hadn't seen in months, startled but still trying to comfort me as she wobbled to her closet repeating, "It's okay, it's okay." I feel guilty about the time I didn't notice that urine had soaked through her pink pajama pants until the hospice nurse arrived and said, "Let's get you cleaned up." I feel guilty that on the morning she died, a beautiful, blue skied April day, I was at work instead of by her side.

Then, of course, there is the guilt I feel about the way I treated others in the aftermath of her death—all of the friendships I let wither or break or never even bloom, all of the love and opportunity I numbly pushed away—and the guilt I feel about the way I treated myself.

I suppose one might reasonably call what I have regret—I

regret not doing more, not being there when she needed me most—but calling it regret ignores my secret and shameful conviction that I am somehow responsible for her suffering, that if I hadn't been so selfish and cruel, things might have turned out differently, or at the least, she might have suffered a little less.

Guilt, I've found, turns you into something simultaneously self-pitying and self-aggrandizing. You feel like a despicable, worthless smudge of a creature at the same time that you endow yourself with an almost superhuman amount of power: If only you'd done this, if only you'd realized that, then everything could have been different in the end. Something, or someone, could have been saved.

During the exorcism of Regan MacNeil, the devil barks at Father Karras, "You killed your mother! You left her alone to die!"

"Shut up!" Father Karras howls back, not because he thinks the devil is wrong, but because he is almost certain that he is right.

•

Guilt and grief are adjacent, but they are not the same. Guilt does not have stages. It moves in circles. To feel guilty is to be forever orbiting the same intrusive thoughts and memories, caught in an endless loop of self-incrimination and shame. *Ruminate* stems from *ruminant,* referring to mammals like cattle, sheep, and deer that chew their regurgitated cud.

Compared to guilt, which is often talked about only in the simplest terms, grief is a subject our culture knows relatively well. Kübler-Ross has colonized grief and turned us all into experts on it. Though we are not necessarily comfortable with grief or accommodating of its extreme mental, physical, or bodily toll, at least we acknowledge that it exists. We accept that the vast majority of humans on this planet will experience it at some point in their lives. The grieving occupy their own special strata in society, however temporarily they may be permitted to stay there. They are to be simultaneously exalted and avoided. Enough books have been written about grief to fill entire stores: books to help you find meaning and strength after loss, books tracing a single author's experience after the death of a loved one, books written to help you connect with others during times of mourning, books to help you better understand grief's ever-shifting contours. Grief is even its own poetic tradition. We have the keen, the threnody, the elegy, the lament.

In *The Year of Magical Thinking,* Joan Didion writes, "Grief turns out to be a place none of us know until we reach it." Didion is right: No amount of cultural representation can possibly prepare you for the lived reality of grief's obliterating dislocation of body, mind, and self. Didion points out that the funeral is often portrayed as grief's weepy pinnacle, whereas anyone who has actually grieved themselves knows that the funeral is little more than an awkward social performance. After it, the bereaved know, grief goes on and on and on.

And yet, even before we've experienced grief ourselves, it is easy to imagine the things we might reasonably do while grieving. How we might cry in the lost one's closet, holding their clothes to our nose, or call their cell phone just so we can hear the sound of their voice on the answering machine. The way grief might sideswipe us out of nowhere, silently and viciously as a subliminal flash, when we are comfortably going about our day—stepping off the curb to cross the street or at a party, laughing, seemingly happily, with a friend. Grief is something so omnipresent that someone who has never experienced intense grief themselves can tell you that you're doing it wrong. I think of the friend who, five years after my mother's death, patted my hand at a bar and, though she had never lost a beloved family member herself, said to me both lovingly and accusingly, "I don't think you have ever *really* grieved your mother."

What this friend didn't understand was that grief was all I was when she met me. I was eighteen when my mother died, trembling and inchoate. At the exact moment I planned to set out for the world of young adulthood and discover what I naively considered my "true self," I was thrust madly and unwillingly into the decimating world of grief. I was too young to have a clear and developed sense of self to fall back on, and so grief became almost all that I was. It hollowed me out and carved me into something I couldn't recognize and didn't want to be, and I stayed that way for years.

Instead of leaving Portland and going away to college like I had always planned, I stayed. I enrolled in a local college and lived at home with my dad and brother, driving the twenty-five minutes back and forth to campus every day, "Both Sides Now" by Joni Mitchell on almost constant repeat. In addition to working part-time at the campus bookstore, I adopted many of the mundane domestic tasks my mother had done when she was alive: grocery shopping, folding laundry, cooking meals. I'd often run into my mother's old friends at the New Seasons Market, women from her prayer group who would corner me in the produce section and cry. To them I was almost invariably curt and cold. I didn't know what to say to them, and I couldn't get away fast enough.

All of my old friends had gone away to college in different towns or states, and as a commuter at a solidly residential school, I wasn't making many new friends either. The sheer act of casually chatting with another student felt fraught and impossible. When I could occasionally summon the wherewithal to socialize, I mostly hung out with a guy from my old high school who had recently returned to Portland after being kicked out of his college for threatening another student with a butter knife while in the middle of a manic episode. We'd hotbox my Jetta until the smoke was almost too dense to see through, and then I'd drive home, study, and cry.

Though I was barely eating anything and obsessively running until my knees ached or swimming laps until I felt faint, my face was constantly puffy and bloated, my stomach oddly distended. In my journals from this period, I regularly describe myself as a "worthless blob." When I looked at myself in the mirror, all I could see was an ugly smear. I fantasized about meeting a handsome boy who would kiss the tears from my cheeks and lift me out of my self-loathing and sorrow. I suspect this was also part of a narrative that had been instilled in me from a very young age by Disney movies and young adult novels: The death of the mother brings about romance and transformation.

This, of course, did not happen. I got along well with my coworker at the bookstore, a kind and handsome Coloradan majoring in environmental studies, but I shut down the moment he started expressing even a vague interest in me. I was terrified. I'd hide from him in the library, call in sick to work so I didn't have to interact with him. After I found myself constitutionally incapable of responding to any of his friendly texts asking me how I was, he changed shifts and never talked to me again.

I can write about this undeniably difficult time with relative ease because there is something like a cultural script for it. It is identifiable. Though in grief I was often pathetic, volatile, and weak, there was the sense that I was, to a point, doing what I was supposed to be doing. I was dutifully passing through those infamous stages that aren't really stages at all but one endless, murky, ever-shifting expanse.

I get tripped up when the guilt comes in. This is where the

narrative splinters, where my certainty frays. I don't know where my grief ends and my guilt begins. I suspect my guilt compounded my grief and perpetuated it to an almost pathological degree, but then again, I don't know what "normal guilt" is supposed to look or feel like. How much of my behavior was not just grief but some twisted form of self-punishment, of penance? Would my grief have been as lasting and as deep if it wasn't compacted by the unshakable suspicion that I could have and should have done more for my mother when she was alive? Where am I supposed to put all this guilt when the person I seek atonement from is no longer alive? Clarity never comes, and I'm left flailing in a narrative void, beaten back by silence and shame.

This is why I am grateful for *The Exorcist,* a major cinematic works that dares to confront the comingling of grief and guilt in all its raw, debilitating intensity. Father Karras is a man who considers himself beyond forgiveness, who has no use for the holy confessional and its promise of eternal reconciliation. I recognize the way Father Karras's mother appears to him after her death, staring at him from the bed with cloudy-eyed recrimination, a recrimination that, because Karras is the one bringing her back to life again and again in his mind, doesn't really belong to her at all.

James Baldwin also considered guilt the overriding but largely unspoken theme of *The Exorcist.* In *The Devil Finds Work,* he describes the ways Satan plays upon Father Karras's guilt as well as Chris MacNeil's guilt over "her failed marriage, her star status, her ambition, her relation to her daughter, her essentially empty and hypocritical and totally unanchored life: in a word, her emancipation." He adds, "this uneasy, and even terrified guilt is the subtext of *The Exorcist,* which cannot, however, exorcise it since it never confronts it. . . . This confrontation would have been to confront the devil."

The devil, Baldwin then argues, resides in each of us, and until we are all ready to confront it, until we encounter "the abyss in [our] own soul," we will forever despise and judge the abyss in the soul of another.

•

Guilt can simply mean culpability, the degree to which a person should or could be held responsible for certain vile or unsavory acts. Though it is most often associated with violating some sort of law or moral standard, guilt doesn't have to be meted out by a court to hold lasting power. Guilt can also be imagined, self-inflicted, a mere *feeling* of responsibility or remorse. As the staggering number of wrongful convictions in this country can attest, guilt can also be misplaced, manufactured, or molded to fit the will of the people with the power to impose it.

Why exactly is our culture so unwilling to talk about guilt—be it guilt imposed by a court of law, one's community, or one's self—in any meaningful or nuanced way? Why does it often feel like I am the only person I know who has ever behaved badly when confronted with the suffering or humanity of another? Why are people so terrified to admit to and reckon with the harm they've caused, however big or small?

Maybe we talk about guilt less than grief simply because most people are better and kinder than I am: They rise to the situation and do what is right. When they look back on their past actions, they have a clear head. They think, *I did what I was supposed to do. I was loving and kind. I did not contribute to another's pain.*

This, however, strikes me as less of an explanation and more as a failure of individual introspection. Failing to do what is right seems like a feature, not a bug, of being alive in this world, and I can't help but feel bitter annoyance at anyone who can honestly look back at their past self and not feel overcome by some type of debilitating guilt.

So maybe most people are simply less self-critical than I am or more forgiving of their past mistakes. If you are not aware of your own wrongdoing, or if you do not consider what you've done wrong in the first place, then how can you feel guilty about it?

I was raised Catholic after all, told for as long as I can remember that I am a shameful sinner who must perpetually plead for the Lord's forgiveness. I grew up believing that meekness and selflessness were the ultimate virtues, and so maybe I am simply hyperaware of all my subsequent failures to "do what Jesus would have done."

Sometimes, I think my guilt has something to do with the fact that I am a woman and that my inability or unwillingness to be ceaselessly warm, nurturing, and kind is often treated, by certain members of my family in particular, as a defect, a black mark blistering in my soul. My occasional anger, selfishness, and dark moods are often perceived not as normal human behaviors but as failures, as threats, as evidence that there is something deeply wrong with me that is past remedy. Maybe I only feel like "a bad person" because the expectations for goodness that have been set for me are nearly impossible to achieve.

When you get down to it, maybe the reason we are scared to talk about guilt, the reason why I hesitate to admit my powerful feelings of guilt to anyone, is not because guilt is less common than grief but because guilt is considered a dirty, unforgiveable thing. Grief passes. Guilt marks you for life. Once you've done a "bad thing," it will define you forever. The only way to free yourself from it, we think, is to throw yourself out a window like Father Karras.

We like to imagine the narrative of guilt as something sim-

ple and clean when in reality it is thorny and complex. Culpability does not reside solely within the individual. It spans out
to family, community, environment, country. Rather than, for
example, a clear line from individual action to legal conviction to righteous and perpetual punishment, guilt is an enor-
mous and tangled web of agency and context. Are individuals
responsible for their own actions and destinies, or are they
inevitably influenced by the world around them? The answer,
of course, is both. We are all, to an extent, both victims and
perpetrators alike.

We don't want to accept that we are agents in bigger frame-
works, that so much of "free will" is in fact predetermined.
Doing so would mean admitting that none of us are as good or
as powerful as we like to think we are.

•

About a week before my mother died, I dreamt that someone
was calling out my name from down a long, echoing hallway.
Marly, Marly, the voice said. At first, it sounded indiscernible
and far away, like a whisper coming from no one. But then
the voice got closer and became clearer. *Marly, Marly,* it said
again.

It was unmistakable: It was the voice of my mother, weak
and muddled but undeniably hers.

I was then jolted awake by a loud thud. I sat up in bed, my
eyes adjusting to the darkness. I turned and looked through the
space of my half-open door, through the very same opening I
used to stare out all night long, waiting for Linda Blair to rush
up the stairs in a backbend and come for me. I saw a slumped
figure sitting cross-legged in the hallway, lit from the moon's
glow pouring in through the skylight above.

I lay in bed staring at it for a few moments before I realized it was my mother. I hadn't been dreaming. She really had

been calling out my name and now she was there, sitting cross-legged in the middle of the hallway in the dead of night.

I leapt out of bed and ran to her.

"Mom," I said urgently, kneeling down beside her and taking her hand. It was the only time in my life I've ever considered slapping myself like they do in the movies to prove you aren't dreaming. But when I touched her, when I felt her cold, clammy palm, I knew I was awake.

"I fell," she said weakly.

"I know," I replied.

I tried to lift her body up, but she was too heavy, slack yet somehow full of lead. I stumbled back, tried one more time, and still couldn't do it. Her head bobbed on her neck like a toy. Her left eye was clouded over. She wasn't wearing any pants.

"Wait here," I said, which was a stupid thing to say, I guess, because where was she going to go?

I woke my dad, and he helped me lift my mother and carry her back to bed. I hovered in their darkened doorway for a few moments before returning to my room. I cried for several hours and then fell asleep.

•

Recently, I logged onto Facebook after many months away and was met with a photograph of my family taken the summer before my eighteenth birthday. It was one of Facebook's automated reminders letting me know that I had uploaded the photo to the site ten years before, when I was studying abroad in Spain.

In the photo, my father, mother, brother, and I are all smiling side by side in front of the silver statue near Portland's famous "Big Pink" building, a giant skyscraper tinted pink and home to one of the city's fanciest restaurants. I'm tan and skinny and young, with red-blond hair that reaches almost to my navel. Sunglasses sit atop my mother's head, and she is wearing dark-pink lipstick. I'd captioned the photograph "Mi Familia."

A few of my friends had commented on the picture shortly after I posted it. Beneath their comments was a message from my brother, Charley. When I scrolled down to read his comment, however, I realized that it wasn't in fact written by him but by my mother.

"Hi Marly," it says. "I liked this pic of all of us, I miss you, I forget how beautiful you are, Mar I am proud that you are mine. Love Mom."

My mother must have saw the post while going through my Facebook when I was away in Spain. She didn't have a Facebook account herself—I'm not sure if many parents had Facebook accounts in 2010—so my guess is that she'd asked Charley if she could log on to his account to see what I was up to in Europe and then had felt inspired to leave a comment herself.

I'm sure I barely paid attention to this comment when she first left it, but when I saw it a decade later, I immediately burst into tears. It was a direct message from my mother, immaculately preserved by the algorithm for ten years. I found myself feeling a warped kind of gratitude toward the tech giant. I am not the type of person to look back through my old photos; I never would have found the message had Facebook not decided to display the photograph and had I not decided to check my account on the exact day I'd posted it a decade before. If I think about it enough, the whole thing almost takes on a spiritual dimension. I can almost convince myself that there are forces, divine or other, pushing my mother and I together, even after so long apart.

In many ways, my extreme guilt about my mother has

endowed me with all of the power and left her with none. In my guilt, I have turned my mother into a kind of helpless child at the mercy of my overblown adolescent cruelty and angst. My guilt has kept the worst parts of her, and of myself, alive. I saw us as two sad and dueling characters in some Sirkian melodrama: her the trembling, all-sacrificing mother, and me the heartless daughter who abandoned her mother to build her own selfish and empty life.

Neither, of course, is fully true.

I think my mother knew exactly what she was doing when she left that comment for me all those years ago. She wasn't necessarily speaking to my eighteen-year-old self, who was busy drinking *calimochos* in Salamanca, traveling to Granada for the weekend, and dancing with strange men in horrible discotheques, but to a future self who might read the note a decade later and finally appreciate and understand its love, and maybe even feel some of that love for herself.

I don't have many wise words to say to those suffering in guilt's torturous grasp, only that if enough time passes, you may start to look a little differently at the memories that haunt you. They will likely continue to play on loop in your mind, and they may still sometimes make you wince or gasp or cry, but you may also begin to see your past self with tenderness and compassion instead of just self-loathing and shame.

I tell myself this:

You sat by your mother's side. You held her hand. When she came to find you in the middle of the night, you rose to meet her.

•

I don't dream of my mother anymore. In a way, I almost wish I did. Even in such dreadful nightmares, at least she was there, visiting me in my sleep.

One day, though, I know she'll return.

When she does, her auburn hair will be long and full and gleaming. She'll have that brilliant smile on her face that radiated good will and light, the smile that made everyone around her feel instantly warm and loved. We'll meet in daylight on some busy city street, walking toward each other through the exhaust and the crowds. We'll approach tentatively at first, worried that any moment the other might turn around and flee. But before we can, she'll reach out her soft and slender hand to mine. I'll take it, and we'll fold into each other's arms, everything forgiven.

Part 5

✛

CONCLUDING PRAYER
OF THANKS

ACKNOWLEDGMENTS

Thank you to Kristen Elias Rowley and the wonderful team at Mad Creek Books for taking on this project and giving it a home alongside so many other amazing essay collections. Thank you to the Tin House Winter Workshop and Rob Spillman for giving me faith in the project at its earliest and messiest stages. Thank you to Elena Passarello for helping me to transform what was a shapeless jumble of words and ideas into something resembling a coherent collection. Thank you Hedgebrook for ten beautiful days on Whidbey Island. Thank you to the *Yale Review* for publishing a version of "My Mother and *The Exorcist*" online. Thank you to all the incredible film writers and critics that taught and radicalized me along the way: Robin Wood, Mark Kermode, Carol J. Clover, Robin R. Means Coleman, Molly Haskell, and so many others. Thank you to my partner, Andre, for reminding me that I am neither good nor evil but a true neutral. Thank you to the many wonderful dogs who brought me endless joy while writing this book: Miles, Danny, Ziggy, and Pepper. Thank you to my brother Charley for spending an incalculable number of hours watching movies with me, talking about them, and planning what to watch next. Thank you for always indulging my wild theories, and for rolling the joints. Thank you to my dad for your love and support. And thank you to the person who inspired this book and who continues to inspire me every day: my mom. Writing this was a way of staying close to you.

SOURCES

Mercedes McCambridge Eats a Raw Egg

Abramovitch, Seth, host. "William Friedkin: *The Exorcist.*" Produced by Chris Pope. *It Happened in Hollywood,* from the *Hollywood Reporter.* October 1, 2018. https://podcasts.apple.com/us/podcast/it-happened-in-hollywood/id1437795866.

Jones, Nick Freand, director. *The Fear of God: 25 Years of The Exorcist.* 1998. TV movie.

"Mercedes McCambridge, 87, Actress Known for Strong Rolls." *New York Times,* March 18, 2004. https://www.nytimes.com/2004/03/18/arts/mercedes-mccambridge-87-actress-known-for-strong-roles.html.

Mortiz, Gwen. "Markle to Mother: 'Thanks for All Your Help.'" *Arkansas Business,* September 30, 2002. https://www.arkansasbusiness.com/article/57608/markle-to-mother-thanks-for-all-your-help.

Pruden, William. "John Lawrence Markle 1941–1987." *Encyclopedia of Arkansas,* edited by Guy Lancaster. Last updated September 9, 2021. https://encyclopediaofarkansas.net/entries/john-lawrence-markle-8000/.

Riddle, Brandon. "Murders on Main." *Arkansas Online.* https://www.arkansasonline.com/murdersonmain/.

My Mother and *The Exorcist*

Ackroyd, Peter. *Alfred Hitchcock: A Brief Life.* Nan A. Talese, 2016.

Bozzuto, James. "Cinematic Neurosis following 'The Exorcist.' Report on four cases." *Journal of Nervous Mental Disorders*, vol. 141, July 1975.

Ebert, Roger. "The Exorcist (2000 Version)." Review. *Chicago Sun Times*, September 22, 2000.

The Johnny Carson Show. "Fernando Lamas/Richard Pryor/Robyn Hilton/William Peter Blatty." *YouTube*. Video. 1:01:01. January 17, 1974. https://www.youtube.com/watch?v=JLkl6NQiJqQ.

Kael, Pauline. "The Exorcist—Review by Pauline Kael." *Scraps from the Loft*, January 11, 2018. https://scrapsfromtheloft.com/movies/the-exorcist-review-by-pauline-kael/#:~:text=It's%20faithful%20not%20to%20the,senseless%20ugliness%20of%20the%20conception. Originally published in the *New Yorker*, 1974.

Kermode, Mark. *The Exorcist*. Revised 2nd ed., British Film Institute, 2003, pp. 8, 9, 10, 68, 72, 76, 84–86.

Rich, Adrienne. *Of Woman Born: Motherhood as Experience and Institution*. Bantam Books, 1976, p. 240.

Sontag, Susan. *Illness and Metaphor and AIDS and Its Metaphors*. Anchor Books, 1978, p. 57.

Wood, Robin. "An Introduction to the American Horror Film." *Robin Wood on the Horror Film: Collected Essays and Reviews*, edited by Barry Keith Grant, Wayne State University Press, 2018, pp. 82, 102.

Excavation

Abramovitch, Seth, host. "William Friedkin: *The Exorcist*." Produced by Chris Pope. *It Happened in Hollywood*, from the *Hollywood Reporter*. October 1, 2018. https://podcasts.apple.com/us/podcast/it-happened-in-hollywood/id1437795866.

Ascher, Rodney, director. *Room 237*. IFC Films, 2012.

Biskind, Peter. *Easy Riders, Raging Bulls: How the Sex, Drugs, and Rock 'n' Roll Generation Saved Hollywood*. Simon & Schuster, 1998, pp. 17, 23, 217, 218, 415.

Blatty, William Peter. *The Exorcist*. Harper & Row, 1971, pp. 6, 7.

———. *If There Were Demons Then Perhaps There Were Angels*. Macmillan, 1998, pp. 6–10, 27, 45, 75.

Brinkley, Bill. "Priest Faces Mt. Rainer Boy Reportedly Held in Devil's Grip." *Washington Post*, August 20, 1949. https://www.

washingtonpost.com/wp-srv/style/longterm/movies/features/
dcmovies/exorcism1949.htm.

Dyer, Geoff. *Zona: A Book About a Film About a Journey to a Room.*
Vintage, 2012, p. 31.

Kermode, Mark. *The Exorcist.* Revised 2nd ed., British Film Institute,
2003, pp. 15, 21, 94–96, 111.

King, Susan. "William Peter Blatty Reflects on 40th Anniversary of *The
Exorcist.*" *Los Angeles Times,* October 8, 2013. https://www.
latimes.com/entertainment/movies/moviesnow/la-et-mn-william-
peter blatty-exorcist-20131008-story.html.

Vitello, Paul. "William Peter Blatty, Author of 'The Exorcist,' Dies at
89." *New York Times,* January 13, 2017. https://www.nytimes.
com/2017/01/13/books/william-peter-blatty-author-of-the-exorcist-
dies-at-89.html?searchResultPosition=1.

Wood, Robin. "An Introduction to the American Horror Film." *Robin
Wood on the Horror Film: Collected Essays and Reviews,* edited by
Barry Keith Grant, Wayne State University Press, 2018, p. 79.

The Loud Silence

Bickel, Christopher. "The Terrifying Rejected 'Exorcist' Soundtrack
the Director Literally Threw out a Window." *Dangerous Minds,*
January 26, 2016. https://dangerousminds.net/comments/terrifying_
rejected_exorcist_soundtrack_the_director_literally_threw_ou.

Biskind, Peter. *Easy Riders, Raging Bulls: How the Sex, Drugs, and
Rock 'n' Roll Generation Saved Hollywood.* Simon & Schuster,
1998, p. 221.

Breznican, Anthony. "The Exorcist: 10 Creepy Details from the Scariest Movie Ever Made." *Entertainment Weekly,* October 31, 2012.
https://ew.com/movies/2012/10/31/the-exorcist-10-creepy-details/.

Kermode, Mark. *The Exorcist.* Revised 2nd ed., British Film Institute,
2003, pp. 48, 111.

Key, Wilson Bryan. *Media Sexploitation: The Hidden Implants in
America's Mass Media—and How They Program and Condition
Your Subconscious Mind.* Prentice Hall, 1976.

———. *Subliminal Seduction: Ad Media's Manipulation of a Not So
Innocent America.* Prentice Hall, 1973.

Lester, Paul. "Mike Oldfield: 'We Wouldn't Have Had Tubular Bells without Drugs.'" *The Guardian,* March 20, 2014. https://www. theguardian.com/music/2014/mar/20/mike-oldfield-interview-tubular-bells-drugs.

Magical Mirrors

Abramovitch, Seth, host. "William Friedkin: *The Exorcist.*" Produced by Chris Pope. *It Happened in Hollywood,* from the *Hollywood Reporter.* October 1, 2018. https://podcasts.apple.com/us/podcast/ it-happened-in-hollywood/id1437795866.

Ager, Rob. "The Even Darker Underbelly of *The Exorcist*-Film Analysis." *YouTube.* Video. 00:27:33. January 4, 2017. https://www. youtube.com/watch?v=BlLrD1CC5wQ.

Boorstein, Michelle. "Vatican Responds to Georgetown Petition by 'Exorcist' author William Peter Blatty." *Washington Post,* May 13, 2014. https://www.washingtonpost.com/national/on-faith/exorcist-author-william-peter-blatty-to-sue-georgetown-university-in-catholic-court/2012/05/18/gIQA90GIZU_story.html.

Clark, Josh, and Charles Bryant, hosts and creators. "The 'Satanic Panic' of the 1980s." *Stuff You Should Know,* from *iHeart Radio.* January 5, 2016. https://www.iheart.com/podcast/105-stuff-you-should-know-26940277/episode/the-satanic-panic-of-the-1980s-29467671/.

Cohen, Nancy. "Why America Has Never Had Universal Child Care." *New Republic,* April 23, 2013. https://newrepublic.com/ article/113009/child-care-america-was-very-close-universal-day-care.

Haskell, Molly. *From Reverence to Rape: The Treatment of Women in the Movies,* 2nd ed., University of Chicago Press, 1987, pp. 24, 323.

Indie Film Hustle. "Martin Scorsese: Alice Doesn't Live Here Anymore—The Director's Series." *YouTube.* Video. 00:11:14. November 1, 2021. https://www.youtube.com/watch?v=6BhIbMA9NJA.

King, Stephen. *Danse Macabre.* Hodder & Stoughton, May 8, 2006.

Later with Bob Costas. "Ellen Burstyn Discusses Exorcist + Alice Doesn't Live Here Anymore." *YouTube.* Video. 00:18:43. June 24, 2021. https://www.youtube.com/watch?v=Sjr6jIhE6iY.

Lee, Benjamin. "Ellen Burstyn: Women on Screen Were Prostitutes or Victims—I Wanted to Embody a Hero." *The Guardian,* April 26, 2018. http://www.theguardian.com/film/apr/26/ellen-burstyn-women-on-screen-were-prostitues-or-victims-i-wanted-to-embody-a-hero.

Lucca, Violet, editor and moderator. "Women in New Hollywood." *The Film Comment Podcast,* from *Film Comment,* February 7, 2017. https://www.filmcomment.com/blog/film-comment-podcast-women-new-hollywood/.

Renfro, Paul. *Stranger Danger: Family Values, Childhood, and the American Carceral State.* Oxford University Press, 2020, p. 15.

Rivera, Geraldo, creator. "Devil Worship: Exposing Satan's Underground." *Geraldo,* Tribute Entertainment. YouTube. Video 00:14:47. 1988. https://www.youtube.com/watch?v=qocBf3_mmic.

Suddath, Claire. "How High Child Care Costs Follow Women Throughout Their Lives." *Bloomberg,* November 18, 2021. https://www.bloomberg.com/news/newsletters/2021-11-18/why-child-care-in-the-u-s-is-broken-for-parents-and-providers.

Something Sharp

Blatty, William Peter. *The Exorcist.* Harper & Row, 1971, p. 190.

Britton, Andrew. *Britton on Film: The Complete Film Criticism of Andrew Britton.* Wayne State University Press, 2008, pp. 232–37.

Calderone, Mary S. "Above and Beyond Politics: The Sexual Socialization of Children." *Pleasure and Danger: Exploring Female Sexuality,* edited by Carol S. Vance, p. 133.

Clover, Carol. *Men, Women, and Chain Saws: Gender in the Modern Horror Film.* Princeton University Press, 1992, p. 102.

David, Jessel, reporter. "Midweek: Linda Blair Promoting The Exorcist in London." *Midweek.* YouTube. Video. 00.09.49. March 27, 1974. March 25, 2014. https://www.youtube.com/watch?v=eb66hGRBf-Q.

Firestone, Shulamith. *The Dialectic of Sex.* Bantam Books, 1970, p. 72.

"Four Decades On, *The Exorcist* is Still a Head-Turner." *All Things Considered,* from *NPR.* October 31, 2013. https://www.npr.org/2013/10/31/241919527/four-decades-on-the-exorcist-still-a-head-turner.

iLoveDogsInc. "I Love Dogs Presents Hollywood Heroes—Linda Blair." *YouTube.* Video. 00:04:01. September 2, 2011. https://www.youtube.com/watch?v=a5g1BrvPPGQ.

James, Rick. *Glow: The Autobiography of Rick James.* Atria, December 29, 2015.

Jones, Nick Freand, director. *The Fear of God: 25 Years of The Exorcist.* 1998. TV Movie.

Kael, Pauline. "The Exorcist—Review by Pauline Kael." *Scraps from the Loft,* January 11, 2018. https://scrapsfromtheloft.com/movies/the-exorcist-review-by-pauline-kael/#:~:text=It's%20faithful%20not%20to%20the,senseless%20ugliness%20of%20the%20conception. Originally published in the *New Yorker,* 1974.

Kermode, Mark. *The Exorcist.* Revised 2nd ed., British Film Institute, 2003, pp. 60, 73.

Levine, Elena. *Wallowing in Sex: The New Sexual Culture of 1970s Television.* Duke University Press, January 9, 2007, pp. 84–89.

"Linda Blair and 31 Held in Drug Case." *New York Times,* December 21, 1977. https://www.nytimes.com/1977/12/21/archives/linda-blair-and-31-held-in-drug-case.html.

"Linda Blair in the Academy Awards." *YouTube.* Video. 00:01:52. January 13, 2015. https://www.youtube.com/watch?v=qDMR02dmwc4.

Millett, Kate. "Beyond Politics: Children and Sexuality?" *Pleasure and Danger: Exploring Female Sexuality,* edited by Carol S. Vance, p. 217.

Mintz, Morton. "Worries about TV Violence Persist." *Washington Post,* August 14, 1978. https://www.washingtonpost.com/archive/politics/1978/08/14/worries-about-tv-violence-persist/ceeo1eo5-875e-4a1c-99a5-b2f1b170do71/.

Nelson, Maggie. *The Argonauts.* Graywolf Press, 2015, p. 66.

"READ: Christine Blasey Ford's Opening Statement for Senate Hearing." *NPR,* September 26, 2018. https://www.npr.org/2018/09/26/651941113/read-christine-blasey-fords-opening-statement-for-senate-hearing.

RuPaul's Drag Race. "Scream Queens." Season 6, episode 3. World of Wonder, March 10, 2014.

Sacks, Ethan. "Possession Is 9/10ths of Linda Blair's Career." *New York Daily News,* November 9, 2006. https://www.nydailynews.com/archives/entertainment/possession-9-10ths-linda-blair-career-article-1.569904. Page discontinued.

Thomas, DeShawn. "How The Exorcist Transformed Linda Blair Forever." *Slash Film.* February 4, 2022. https://www.slashfilm.com/758106/how-the-exorcist-transformed-linda-blair-forever/#:~:text=

After%20his%20declaration%20that%20the,her%20participation
%20in%20the%20movie.

Wood, Robin. "An Introduction to the American Horror Film." *Robin Wood on the Horror Film: Collected Essays and Reviews,* edited by Barry Keith Grant, Wayne State University Press, 2018, p. 85.

———. "Der Erlkönig: The Ambiguities of Horror." *Robin Wood on the Horror Film: Collected Essays and Reviews,* edited by Barry Keith Grant, Wayne State University Press, 2018, p. 111.

James Baldwin Sees *The Exorcist* in 1973

Anderson, Carol. *White Rage: The Unspoken Truth of Our Racial Divide.* Bloomsbury, 2016, pp. 101, 104.

Baldwin, James. *The Devil Finds Work.* Vintage Books. 1976.

Means Coleman, Robin. *Horror Noire: Blacks in the American Horror Film from the 1980s to the Present.* Routledge, 2011.

Museum of the Moving Image. "The First Civil Right." Advertisement archive. 1968. http://www.livingroomcandidate.org/commercials/1968/the-first-civil-right.

Saturday Night Live. "The Exorcist 2 (ft. Richard Pryor)—SNL." YouTube. Video. 00:04:53. October 10, 2013. https://www.youtube.com/watch?v=B8dKnFU5LUE.

Veneman, Jerry. "Abby's Lazarus Soul: William Girdler's Tale of Demon Possession in Search of a New Audience." *Monsterzine,* 2002. http://monsterzine.com/200204/abby.php.

The Priests of My Youth

Gottlieb, Sidney, editor. *Alfred Hitchcock: Interviews.* University Press Mississippi, 2003, p. 56.

Kermode, Mark. *The Exorcist.* Revised 2nd ed., British Film Institute, 2003, p. 96.

The Operating Theater

Abramovitch, Seth, host. "William Friedkin: *The Exorcist.*" Produced by Chris Pope. *It Happened in Hollywood,* from the *Hollywood*

Reporter. October 1, 2018. https://podcasts.apple.com/us/podcast/
it-happened-in-hollywood/id1437795866.

Derry, Charles. *Dark Dreams 2.0: A Psychological History of the Modern Horror Film.* McFarland & Company, 2009, pp. 105, 333.

Eakins, Thomas. *The Agnew Clinic.* 1989. Oil on canvas. Philadelphia Museum of Art, Philadelphia. https://archives.upenn.edu/exhibits/penn-history/class-histories/medical-class-of-1889/agnew-clinic/.

Farago, Jason. "Taking Lessons from a Bloody Masterpiece." *New York Times,* May 28, 2020. https://www.nytimes.com/interactive/2020/05/28/arts/design/thomas-eakins-gross-clinic.html.

Kermode, Mark. *The Exorcist.* Revised 2nd ed., British Film Institute, 2003, p. 53.

Miller, Matt. "Searching for the Truth About the Actual Murderer in *The Exorcist.*" *Esquire,* October 25, 2018. https://www.esquire.com/entertainment/movies/a23724262/paul-bateson-the-exorcist-murderer-true-story/.

Mukherjee, Siddhartha. *The Emperor of All Maladies: A Biography of Cancer.* Scribner, 2010, p. 181.

Sontag, Susan. *Illness as Metaphor* and *Aids and Its Metaphors.* Doubleday, 1978, p. 43.

Father Karras Dreams of His Mother

Baldwin, James. *The Devil Finds Work.* Vintage Books, 1976, p. 124.

Blatty, William Peter. *The Exorcist.* Harper & Row, 1971, p. 86.

Didion, Joan. *The Year of Magical Thinking.* Knopf, 2005, p. 58.

21st CENTURY ESSAYS
David Lazar and Patrick Madden, Series Editors

This series from Mad Creek Books is a vehicle to discover, publish, and promote some of the most daring, ingenious, and artistic nonfiction. This is the first and only major series that announces its focus on the essay—a genre whose plasticity, timelessness, popularity, and centrality to nonfiction writing make it especially important in the field of nonfiction literature. In addition to publishing the most interesting and innovative books of essays by American writers, the series publishes extraordinary international essayists and reprint works by neglected or forgotten essayists, voices that deserve to be heard, revived, and reprised. The series is a major addition to the possibilities of contemporary literary nonfiction, focusing on that central, frequently chimerical, and invariably supple form: The Essay.

*Annual Gournay Prize Winner

*Annual Gournay Prize Winner